PRAISE FOR MIKAELA KINER
AND *FEMALE FIREBRANDS*

"Kiner advocates practicing inclusion in the workplace, saying goodbye to outdated norms where women are often sidelined and excluded, and instead turning everyone—women and men both—into advocates and allies. Kiner argues that the old ways of corporate America—one seat at the table, double standards for women, and motherhood penalties—have prevented women from thriving for far too long. Her practical advice, illustrated by candid stories of her own and of the thirteen female firebrands she interviewed, shows readers a new way to create workplaces where everyone has a sense of belonging."

**—CARA BRENNAN ALLAMANO AND
ROBBY PETERS, Founders, PeopleTech Partners**

"As a seasoned HR veteran, Mikaela Kiner has seen it all. She and the women she interviewed share candid stories about what professional women face every day and how they persevere. Kiner does not hesitate to tackle complex issues of privilege and race. Though these topics will certainly make for some discomfort among readers, the women's unflagging spirit and resiliency are that much more admirable given the hard truths about how far we still are from attaining equality."

—STELLA ASHAOLU, Founder & CEO, WeSolv

"*Female Firebrands* is a beautiful expression of the desire to be better, to strive for more. This book is a positive disruption for any individual or organization looking to create a new way of being. Mikaela offers a meaningful acknowledgment of systemic barriers while pointing out the negative thought patterns and biased practices that keep us from belonging. Through effective storytelling and expert guidance, she pushes us to think bigger and imagine an equitable future where everyone can thrive. Consider this a powerful call to action and a tangible tool for every leader looking to make a change in the world."

—MICHAELA AYERS, Founder, Nourish

"If you want to be inspired by other women's stories, look no further than *Female Firebrands*. This candid, modern, practical, and user-friendly book is a great illustration of the obstacles women face and how to overcome them. Few dispute that inclusion and belonging matter, so why does creating environments that include women continue to elude many companies? This much-needed book offers answers, specific tools, and tips on how to advocate for yourself and other women in ways that count."

—ELIZABETH BASTONI, Independent Director and Consultant

"Mikaela Kiner brilliantly tackles one of the most critical issues in today's society: gender diversity in the workplace. Through an account of her own experience as a longtime Amazon executive and the stories of the women alike, Kiner offers a refreshing and uniquely honest perspective on what it means to be a female in the modern-day workplace. *Female Firebrands* will inspire readers to think critically about the ways in which gender impacts their daily lives and will provide the tools necessary to be advocates for change."

—ANISH BATLAW, Operating Partner, General Atlantic

"*Female Firebrands* is a wonderful book that honors the spirit, passion, and commitment women bring to work, the workplace, and leadership. The stories are inspirational and educational for everyone, and I highly recommend this book for men and women in business."

—JOSH BERSIN, Global Industry Analyst in Leadership and HR

"A smartly written book that puts women's stories at the center of the narrative and will help women (and men) effect positive change in the workplace. I couldn't get enough of these real-life stories told by women from an incredibly diverse set of industries and backgrounds. Their advice and ideas are remarkably easy to understand and put into action. I plan on giving this book to the potential female firebrands I know, and the men that want to be great advocates."

—CHRIS CAPOSSELA, Chief Marketing Officer, Microsoft

"I have spent the past 20 years working as a senior human resource leader in the technology industry. Mikaela's story and the stories of the female firebrands she spotlights are my story and the story of millions of women across the world. These stories provide insight, guidance, and support and are a must-read if you are a woman working in business today, a young woman beginning her career, or anyone who supports women in the workplace. This book will warm your heart, ignite your passion, and foster belief in yourself. Thank you, Mikaela, for sharing these stories and supporting women everywhere."

—REBECCA CLEMENTS, VP of HR at Moz

"Mikaela provides a thought-provoking examination of inequities through tangible, relatable stories that challenge the status quo. Reading this book, I often found myself nodding in agreement and then pausing to question my own privilege and way of thinking."

—AHMAD CORNER, Founder and Community Builder, Young Professionals Organization

"As a Latina and founder of a Circle of Latinas in Seattle, I constantly hear heartbreaking stories about how women of color are discriminated against in the workplace and society. Having someone like Mikaela bringing light to these sorties makes my heart pound faster. So many women who were interviewed for this book have not only been ferocious allies and women's advocates, but also good friends that I admire. I couldn't be prouder to see their voices represented in this book. Mikaela is on a mission of seeing more women breaking the glass ceiling, and this book is all about bringing awareness and more allies to make this happen. This book is a must for everyone who wants to get inspired and desires to understand more about the reality that women face in this society."

—LAURA ESPRIU, Founder of Latinas in Seattle and Laura Espriu Coaching & Consulting

"What I loved about this book was the marriage of deeply personal stories from a diverse group of women with actionable advice for not just women but also male advocates, HR, and business leaders. Without an integrated approach to tackling inequities in the workplace, nothing will improve. Mikaela Kiner makes a call for all of us to examine and check our own privileges and then to use those same privileges to help create a more equitable workplace for everyone."

—LYDIA FRANK, VP of Content Strategy, PayScale

"In her new book, Mikaela Kiner provides a fresh, concise, and authoritative account of the challenges women leaders face in today's corporate and entrepreneurial work environments. She weaves together the stories of 13 inspiring women, who provide unique perspectives on how the modern workplace must evolve to become a more balanced, inclusive, and empowering place. Male managers like me who aspire to be more conscious, curious, and thoughtful about our roles, biases, and team cultures will find practical advice in Kiner's work for becoming stronger advocates for women and better leaders. Kiner's interviews are peppered with insightful commentary and data, as well as checklists at the end of each chapter to help put wisdom into action. Kiner's work is a welcome addition to the literature on women in the workplace and a fun, fascinating read!"

—DAVEY FRIEDMAN, Consumer Sales Manager, WeWork

"Women in recent decades have become more powerful and effective advocates—for themselves and for other women. Advocacy takes confidence, commitment, and yes, the attitude of a firebrand—someone who sets off sparks that kindle change. *Female Firebrands* adds something essential to the conversation because it not only profiles women who fearlessly push for change, but it also offers clear and actionable tactics that every woman can use to more powerfully advocate for what she and others need. Women's engagement will be a key resource for creating a workplace that works for everyone. *Female Firebrands* helps show us how to get there."

—SALLY HELGESEN, Author, *How Women Rise*,
The Female Advantage*, and *The Female Vision

"As a leader of a team or organization, whether you are a woman or man, *Female Firebrands* is a practical read of some very complicated topics. It is an honest look at many important issues facing our workforce. Mikaela is one of the highest-judgment people I've had the pleasure to work with, and she applies that horsepower to an unflinching dive into traditionally sensitive topics with the goal of making them normalized, accessible, and actionable. At the end of every chapter is a checklist (for women, male advocates, and HR professionals) that is both practical and enormously helpful. Whether you are a longtime leader or a new leader, *Female Firebrands* is a must-read for today's leaders seeking to understand and do right."

—JERRY HUNTER, SVP Engineering, Snap Inc.

"Kiner's *Female Firebrands* demonstrates that in the modern workplace, there must be a better way—that Mikaela shows us in an actionable and unapologetic manner. Kiner illustrates her guidance with compelling examples of women in the workplace and follows up with tangible, tactical how-to steps at the end of each chapter. Whether you're an industry veteran, fresh out of school, or returning after a break, this is a must-have survival handbook for women in the corporate workplace."

—NANCY JENSEN, CEO and Co-Founder, The Swing Shift

"I dare anyone to read the introduction (the author's story) and not want to immediately dive into this book. It is not easy to sum up an interview, especially with the caliber of women selected. So much happens in that conversation that can hardly be captured. The author does it artfully. Bravo. Tip to all readers: use this book as a great conversation sparker for a group of friends. Read one or two stories and just talk about the impact of that story on you and your personal "take-aways." I bet one meeting will lead to another. Support for our growth is out there—it just comes in all shapes and sizes. This is one way of getting and giving that support! The author modeled bravery, authenticity, smarts, incisiveness, inclusion, as well as warmth and humor in her story. You can skip many introductions—don't skip this one! Bravo Mikaela! I loved that the stories shared by the author were so well done. Short, memorable, honest, and authentic. They immediately touched me. There are so many lessons buried in each story and so many moments of learning. Start anywhere and go anywhere . . . you'll love the journey."

—BEVERLY KAYE, 2018 ATD Lifetime Achievement
Award Winner and Author, *Help Them Grow or Watch*
Them Go** and *Love 'Em or Lose 'Em

"*#FemaleFirebrands* offers authentic insight into our evolving workplace, as the rules are getting rewritten in real time. It also gives insight into what it takes to simultaneously balance ambition and commitment to your family. It is modern and honest. A must-read for today's career trailblazer."

—JAIME KLEIN, Founder, Inspire HR

"Mikaela's book is soothing for the soul. After 35 years in the workplace with feelings that overwhelm with snippets of hope, I think that this book supports understanding today's issues with an insightful, direct, and compassionate message. As a white woman and a beneficiary of the diversity movement, I particularly appreciate the discussion of my white privilege and what I need to do to be more of an advocate and inclusive of all women. The suggestions in regard to each topic feel completely relevant, and gathered from inspiring 'firebrands,' they demonstrate Mikaela's value for collaboration, inclusivity, and the acknowledgment of the gifts of other women."

—JOY LEACH, President of PRI Leadership and Master Certified Coach, Hudson Institute Leadership Team

"*Female Firebrands* is filled with inspiring stories and practical wisdom about how to be braver in speaking up for ourselves and for others. In the 1980s, one of my early mentors—a man—taught me to have the courage of my convictions. That advice is as important today as it ever was. Mikaela's book will help all of us have the courage of our convictions and create workplaces that are more whole, inclusive, and vibrant."

—SUSAN MANN, Leadership & Career Coach, Facilitator, and Consultant

"As a woman and a venture capitalist, I've been fortunate to find myself in a position to advocate for women, especially female founders. While reading *Female Firebrands* you'll learn what I know to be true—equity and inclusion at work lead to more collaboration and better business outcomes. What's groundbreaking about Kiner's book is how the firebrands candidly share their stories about what's held them back and how they've succeeded. *Female Firebrands* is the new playbook that will encourage and inspire you to improve the future of work for yourself and women everywhere."

—AMY MCCULLOUGH, President and Managing Director at Trilogy Equity Partners

"I can't imagine a better person than Mikaela Kiner to write a book that positively addresses the reality of what it means to be a woman in corporate America. Reading the brutally honest experiences of women who've 'been there,' coupled with realistic advice on how to improve not only your own experience at work, but also that of others, is extremely empowering. I've been fortunate to have Mikaela as a friend and colleague who has provided valuable guidance and advice as I've progressed in my career; I'm thrilled that she has used her expertise to offer similar guidance through this book to working women everywhere!"

—TERESA MILLER, General Counsel, *Rick Steves' Europe*

"In her book *Female Firebrands*, Mikaela Kiner directly tackles challenges of women in the workplace. By bringing in a diverse set of female firebrand voices and interweaving them with in-depth research and her own wisdom and experience, Mikaela gives us a book that both illuminates our challenges in new ways and provides a pragmatic playbook not just for women, but also HR professionals and men advocates."

—SABINA NAWAZ, Global CEO Coach, Keynote Speaker, and Writer for *Harvard Business Review* **and** *Forbes*

"We all need to be louder in the fight for gender equity in the workplace, and Kiner keenly provides techniques to do just that. This book thoughtfully rounds up real women's stories and, most importantly, guides all of us in doing better. A must-read for anyone working toward a better professional future for women."

—AMY NELSON, Founder & CEO, The Riveter

"Reading *Female Firebrands* is like getting to listen to a private conversation among powerful, smart women sharing their war stories about the challenges of being a woman in the workplace. Kiner is personable, authentic, and pragmatic. The book combines inspiration with actionable advice targeted not only to female professionals, but also to men who want to be better advocates and HR and business leaders who want to lead better."

—JULIE PHAM, VP of Community Engagement & Marketing, Washington Technology Industry Association

"A frank, straightforward examination of what women face in the workplace on a daily basis. Mikaela incorporates stories from a strong cross-section of women, with up-to-the-minute examples that made me ache with empathy, grind my teeth in indignation, and applaud the courage of women everywhere who are choosing to stand up to change the workplace for themselves—and for all of us."

—AMY SALLIN, Director at the Buerk Center for Entrepreneurship

"Female Firebrands provides an honest account of women's experience in corporate America as it has been—and offers a clear, tangible path toward what it must become. Incorporating diverse perspectives from women across the whole spectrum of work, the book discusses ideas and strategies for both men and women to create an empowered, inclusive workplace for all women. Mikaela's passion, pragmatism, and authenticity shines through, making this a must-have handbook for everyone in the corporate world."

—MANMEET SANDHU, Chief People Officer, PhonePe

"In *Female Firebrands: Stories and Techniques to Ignite Change, Take Control, and Succeed in the Workplace*, CEO and executive coach Mikaela Kiner blends her story with the stories of the female firebrands she interviewed. These mission-driven women ranging from CEOs and founders to diversity experts and nonprofit leaders share their struggles and achievements and talk about the power of women supporting women. With both candor and optimism, Kiner provides the tips—and encouragement—that women and male advocates need so they can work together toward lasting change."

—ELIZABETH SCALLON, Head of WeWork Labs Northwest

"A candid should-read by Michaela Kiner about her story and those of 13 other powerhouse women! *Female Firebrands* is recommended reading for all women and men who want to be change agents for true gender equality for ALL women in the workplace."

—TAMA SMITH, Former CEO of The Tyra Banks Company and the leader of Women Living A Richer Life at Brighton Jones

"If companies want to create workplaces that inspire people to do their best work, then we have to face the hard truths people experience today. Mikaela helps us better understand the systemic factors and history at play in many organizations and punctuates this knowledge with the impact that these factors have had on real individuals at all stages of their career. But instead of just highlighting the challenges, *Female Firebrands* provides actions that leaders, individuals, allies, and HR professionals can take to make their organizations more equitable and more human for everyone. Transforming companies into ones our children will be proud to work for will continue to take intentional work at all levels, and Mikaela provides us all with a great field guide to get started wherever you are today."

—DAN SPAULDING, Chief People Officer, Zillow Group

"As a woman leader in a large organization, *Female Firebrands* helped me identify my own strengths as an advocate and champion for the women around me. It gave me even more courage to speak up, along with new tips and techniques that I can use and share with my team. What I love most about the book is Kiner's positive message—it's time for change, and there's no turning back. She's achieved her goal of giving women and men the tools we need to increase inclusion and gender equality at work."

—DEEPTI VARMA, Country Leader HR - Amazon India and MENA Region (Middle East & North Africa)

"As an entrepreneur and woman of color, I can relate to Mikaela Kiner's story and the stories of the women that she highlights in the book. The stories are authentic, heart-warming, and provide so much hope and encouragement for women who continue to become firebrands against all odds."

—MARY-FRANCES WINTERS, President and CEO, The Winters Group, Inc.—a 35-year-old MWBE Diversity, Equity and Inclusion Consulting Firm

FEMALE
FIREBRANDS

Stories *and* Techniques *to* Ignite Change,
Take Control, *and* Succeed *in the* Workplace

FEMALE
FIREBRANDS

Mikaela Kiner

GREENLEAF
BOOK GROUP PRESS

Published by Greenleaf Book Group Press
Austin, Texas
www.gbgpress.com

Distributed by Greenleaf Book Group

For ordering information or special discounts for bulk purchases, please contact Greenleaf Book Group at PO Box 91869, Austin, TX 78709, 512.891.6100.

Design and composition by Greenleaf Book Group
Cover design by Greenleaf Book Group
"Pantoum of the Glass Ceiling" by Sabina Baumgardner. Copyright © 2019 by Sabina Baumgardner. Reproduced by permission of the poet.

Publisher's Cataloging-in-Publication data is available.

Print ISBN: 978-1-62634-673-4
eBook ISBN: 978-1-62634-674-1
Audiobook ISBN: 978-1-62634-700-7

Part of the Tree Neutral® program, which offsets the number of trees consumed in the production and printing of this book by taking proactive steps, such as planting trees in direct proportion to the number of trees used: www.treeneutral.com

TreeNeutral

Printed in the United States of America on acid-free paper

19 20 21 22 23 24   10 9 8 7 6 5 4 3 2 1

First Edition

This book is dedicated to my husband Henry—
my biggest champion, always.

"The original firebrands were incendiary indeed; they were pieces of wood set burning at the fire, perhaps for use as a light or a weapon . . . But the burning embers of the wooden firebrand quickly sparked figurative uses for the term, too . . . by 1382, English writers were using it for anyone who kindled mischief or inflamed passions."[1]

---

1   Merriam-Webster, s.v. "firebrand," accessed February 22, 2019, https://www.merriam-webster.com/dictionary/firebrand

"Right now, when we're hearing so much disturbing and hateful rhetoric, it is so important to remember that our diversity has been—and will always be—our greatest source of strength and pride here in the United States."

—Michelle Obama

CONTENTS

PART TWO: Firebrands Go Face-To-Face with the Issues

ACKNOWLEDGMENTS

This book would not have been possible without the thirteen female firebrands who inspired me and courageously shared their stories. I'm also grateful to the Next Generation women for their participation: Ema Bargeron, Morgan De Lancy, Brigitte Eder, Lydia Huang, Angela Lin, Sandhya Nakhasi, Sage Ke'alohilani Quiamno, Kiana Ting, and Malvika Wadhawan.

Aiko, my guide and collaborator regarding privilege, race, and intersectionality—I could not have broached these important topics without your wisdom. Heartfelt thanks to Erin Donley, my original thought partner, for organizing the interviews into meaningful themes that became the basis for this book. Kudos to Christina Watt for her incisive feedback.

I was lucky to have the two most amazing interns: Allison Bunker, who suggested the Next Gen interviews, and Noelle Nightingale, who conducted extensive research. Both of them brought incredible expertise to the project.

Special thanks to my staff at Reverb: Marlyn Chu, Michelle Fink, Lindsay Foley, Sjohn Jepsen, Hanako Olmer, and Sarah Wilkins for supporting me in balancing this book with my day job. I want to recognize Reverb consultant Adrienne Kortas, creator of The Advocacy Spectrum, for helping all of us become more vocal and proactive advocates.

Thanks to the mentors, sponsors, and allies who have been generous with their time and feedback to help me grow over the course of my career: Shannon Anderson, Robin Andrulevich, Anish Batlaw,

Dave Gartenberg, Abilio Gonzalez, Jerry Hunter, Kathy Lindenbaum Susan Mann, Raj Raghavan, Mala Singh, and many others.

Organizations that foster learning and compassion are rare, and I appreciate those that are part of my life: The Hudson Institute, and Brené Brown's Dare to Lead™ facilitator community. Also Franklin High and Billings Middle School, for teaching our kids to be socially aware, inclusive, and empathetic people and giving them a safe space to learn and grow.

To my parents, who raised me to be decisive, principled, and hard-working. My husband Henry, who proved he really would "follow me anywhere" when we moved our family to South India. My son Simon, who is a quiet feminist, and my daughter Sidonie, who is the most vocal feminist I know.

THE CAREER OF A LIFETIME

E arly in my career, I dreamt of being sent on an international assignment. Experiencing a variety of people, cultures, landscapes, and foods has always intrigued me. When my assumptions are challenged, and when I can see the world through another person's eyes, is when I flourish—personally and professionally.

In 2009, Amazon gave me a chance to take on that international assignment, and it was one of my most incredible life experiences. Hyderabad, India, became our family home. We stayed for three years— my husband, Henry, and our children, Simon and Sidonie (we call her Sido), who were seven and four at the time. People always commented on what a wonderful learning opportunity it was for the kids to experience a different culture, and it was the same for us as adults.

My biggest challenge was that my job as an HR director involved extensive travel. The jaunt to Amazon HQ in Seattle, Washington, was roughly twenty-four hours door-to-door on a good day. I took trips ranging from a few days to a week, traveling to the United States twenty times in three years, and making shorter trips to Bangalore and Chennai (large technology hubs in South India) monthly. Add the inevitable emergency meeting and quarterly team offsites, and you get the picture—work and travel consumed much of my existence.

Thankfully, Henry stayed at home with the kids. This was unheard of for a man in India, and to be culturally accepted, he created a sort of alibi about being on sabbatical and teaching music at the international school. Even though this was true, each time he met someone new, he had to tell the story "just so," in order to avoid confusion. When we explained to locals that my assignment with Amazon brought us to India, many would pause, look at Henry, and say, "But sir, you must also work for Amazon." It was unthinkable that we would move for my job, and not his. But that is a story for another day.

My Seven-Year-Old and the Tipping Point

When we returned to Seattle in June 2012, the temperature was cool, it was drizzling, and the kids were freezing. Summer days in Hyderabad hit a stifling, dry 109 degrees daily, and the winters provided only a two-week reprieve from the heat. Simon and Sidonie didn't recognize American money, and they didn't realize we knew how to drive a car because in India, it's common to hire a local driver. When we left, the kids begged our driver, Akheel, to come home with us. But in spite of everything, Henry and I merged back into American norms as independent drivers, bundled in sweatshirts to protect us from the Pacific Northwest cold.

Moving 10,000 miles, enrolling the kids in school, and settling into temporary housing was no small feat, but before returning to work, I took off only four business days. It's common for returning expats to feel disconnected, and my first day back at Amazon felt chilly and impersonal since the company had changed and grown so much while I was away. I entered my office to find no phone, no coat hook, and no lock on the door. There wasn't even a chair.

I'll never forget the kindness of my friend Kelly Wolf, who welcomed me with a card and a plant. I didn't take others' aloofness personally: after seven years at Microsoft and nearly six years at Amazon, I understood the heavy demands placed on employees at these companies. People were busy, and I got it. The old Amazon tagline was still fresh in my mind: "Work long, hard, and smart. You can't choose two out of three." To their credit, Amazon has focused increasingly on people's well-being in the past few years, in some cases even hosting "work-life harmony" discussions between leaders and employees.

In India, the hours were long, including regular calls at night often lasting until 11:00 p.m. Because I had been in a remote location, I was used to a degree of freedom and control over my work. Now that I was back at headquarters, I missed the ability to move quickly and make my own decisions. Getting back that kind of auton-

> *"You look like a caged animal. Why don't you just go?"*

omy proved to be impossible. I had no staff and four open positions on the team I inherited. Because of the vacancies, I was responsible for 1,300 clients globally with limited support. As I'd been taught all my life, I worked long and hard—and, hopefully, smart too—to make sure my clients got what they needed.

Some of my reintegration efforts included taking my laptop to Starbucks on the weekends, where I could focus without being distracted by the kids or household chores. One Saturday morning the four of us were having breakfast, and though I was home with my family, I wasn't truly present. I had loads of work to do before Monday, and my head was exploding. Henry said, "You look like a caged animal. Why don't you just go?" With his support and encouragement, I was out the door in an instant.

In India, it was normal for me to be gone, but expectations started to shift when we got back to the States. We were all exhausted from the move, and I didn't recognize the toll it had taken—until the first day of the new school year, a few months after our return. Sido had just started second grade, and she was not happy with our new life in

Seattle. From the back of the car, my daughter did something that changed all of our lives. She read me the riot act:

"Mom, why aren't you ever home? Why don't you take me to school? How come only Dad knows my friends' phone numbers?"

I sat silently in disbelief. My seven-year-old daughter had just clearly and pointedly expressed her needs. Until then, a combination of loving adults (her dad, teachers, grandparents, soccer and gymnastics coaches) had always been enough for her. Now, she needed not just those adults; she needed more of me. Sido was right.

I have always known I'm a good, loving parent, and I've never felt guilty about my demanding career. I learned early on, after Simon was born, that sometimes I made sacrifices for work, and other times I made sacrifices for my family. As long as those sacrifices were equally balanced, I had always been able to find a happy medium.

Sido's questions were a wake-up call. My immediate reaction was *She's right. This is absurd. Life's too short. I* should *take her to school. I* should *know her friends' phone numbers. I* should *be there for her more. I* want *to be there. Something has to change.*

Laying Down the Law

A few months later, I made the choice to leave Amazon for a senior HR director role at PopCap Games, a smaller company where I could work fewer hours and still be successful. The move freed up space for family—and for me. For the first time in fifteen years, I was able to invest in myself and focus on my own career growth. I took long walks in the Seattle rain, read *The New Yorker* cover to cover, and enrolled in a leadership coaching program at the Hudson Institute in Santa Barbara. Having time to pursue my interests, to branch out, and not be consumed by my work was more than a relief; it was a lifesaver. I felt like a normal person again. I didn't resent the moms who had time to meet for coffee after dropping their kids off at school. I began to understand how friends and neighbors went about their days at a more leisurely pace.

My last corporate job after leaving PopCap was as VP Human Resources at Redfin. Attaining that job title was a big milestone in a corporate world where people care about such things. The title was important to me simply because it signified that I was a peer to other executives on the leadership team. By then, I'd also become clear about my personal values and boundaries. I shared these when I was being recruited into Redfin, knowing that if our values didn't align, I was prepared to walk away. Point by point, I told my future boss:

> *"I wished someone had warned me in my twenties that not all companies require intense juggling acts and so much sacrifice to make career, life, and family work well together."*

- I'm a committed and hard worker, but I don't work every day, night, and weekend.

- I have an executive coaching practice that I'll be maintaining on the side.

- I show up late on Fridays because I drive my daughter to school.

Redfin graciously accepted my terms, and I remained there for a year. By this time, I was a fifteen-year veteran in human resources who'd spent an extraordinary amount of time "making things work" at various companies. I wished someone had warned me in my twenties that not all companies require intense juggling acts and so much sacrifice to make career, life, and family work well together.

I want to acknowledge here and now that I *chose* these hard-charging companies, and I chose to work as hard as I knew how. I did everything in my power to perform well and not let anyone down. I was driven, and the choices were my own. At the same time, I couldn't help but feel that there was about 25% too much work required in each of the big corporate jobs I had. I reached a breaking point at each company when I felt forced to make a choice. Each time—though the choice was not necessarily easy or obvious—I chose family.

Why Wasn't I Invited?

As someone who believed in the myth of meritocracy, I wish I'd been more prepared for the *microaggressions* and exclusion that can happen at work, especially to women. Being an optimist, I've often felt naive and even blindsided by how underrepresented people are treated. I like to say that I came by my role as an HR professional (now often referred to as "People Operations") honestly.

Both of my parents are employment attorneys on the plaintiff's side, which means they sue companies when people have been harassed or discriminated against at work. I grew up hearing dinner table conversations about sexual harassment, pregnancy discrimination, and other issues that left me thinking there had to be a better way to work together and handle these situations without things getting so out of hand that an attorney was needed. Even today, when I witness inappropriate behavior at work, I wonder why people behave the way they do. Working in HR has given me a unique, up-close view of what goes on in corporate America, and it's not always pretty.

Like others in my generation, I grew up with TV shows, music, and movies that portrayed women through negative stereotypes. At the same time, my mom taught me that becoming Miss Universe was not an appropriate life goal, and we never had a Barbie in our house. The extent to which women and other groups were minimalized in eighties media and entertainment might have seemed like a humorous exaggeration at the time, but thirty-five years later, gender discrimination still exists. The current #MeToo and #TimesUp movements offer glimpses of behavior that is no longer tolerated but has been pervasive for decades.

As my career progressed, I found myself questioning companies whose work hours and reward structures were designed long ago—by and for men. I wondered why I wasn't invited to executive dinners or drinks with the guys, and why I was told to refrain from asking questions in meetings. Even though my questions were relevant, I was told they were disruptive. Frequently the only woman on the executive team, I watched men form what seemed like instant camaraderie while keeping me at arm's length. I saw male peers and executives repeatedly let off the hook for missing meetings, yelling, and name calling, yet I was shut down when all I wanted was to participate and do my job.

Both men and women have been my advocates at times. Over the years, there were also managers who left me angry and confused by their feedback. Surprisingly, some of the most personal and unclear feedback I heard came from female bosses. Many of their critical statements were contradictory and not constructive, like the ones below.

- "You are like a dog with a bone when you have a goal." My boss gave me this feedback in a company culture that was very results oriented. Men all around me were praised and promoted when they stopped at nothing to achieve their goals.

- "You're arrogant." This felt extremely personal, especially when I asked for context and my manager could not provide it. She told me this was the opinion of one of her peers, so I promptly contacted her asking how I could improve. She dismissed it, saying I had been quite direct with one of her team members, but that the person had poor follow-through, so it was understandable. In a culture known for being direct, my drive for results was criticized. Yet when I saw male executives point fingers, yell, and publicly attack people, it was repeatedly excused as "that's just so-and-so," as if the frequency of this behavior made it OK, for men.

- "You're so strategic, people can't understand you," and "You're too tactical to interact with senior leaders." Either of these comments might have been constructive; however, in combination and coming from the same boss at roughly the same time, they were contradictory. I'm not certain what it means to be too strategic, and without specific examples these remarks left me not understanding the problem or how I could work toward a solution.

- "You don't think big enough." I value the idea of thinking big picture and long term. At the same time, it's always possible to think bigger. Without examples of what this looks like in action, who's doing it well, or how to improve, it was too ambiguous to act on.

- "You're not hands-on enough," and "You're too hands-on." Again, both of these remarks could be valid at different times and on different projects. At times I felt I might wake up to one or the other, never knowing which it would be. When the same boss alternates between two extremes, it creates a moving target.

Some people say women simply need to "get over it" and learn to be tough. Don't take things so personally. But when women receive feedback that is not helpful or actionable, it's difficult to move forward. The *double standard* that requires women to be nice but assertive, direct but not aggressive, passionate but not emotional, and so on, has a direct impact on women's ability to succeed. Women are often told to demonstrate opposing behaviors, which only leads to increased confusion about how to grow and which skills they need to focus on.

The Intangibles

As I was, many women are plagued by feedback that is unclear, not actionable, and creates a moving target. They may get conflicting feedback as I did when I was told I was both "too strategic" and "too tactical." If that sounds familiar, you are not alone. A *Thrive Global* article by Jena Booher titled "Too Edgy, Too Nice, Too Much!!" describes this phenomenon:

"Inevitably, at the end of every year during my year-end review, my managers would report I was 'too edgy' and I needed to pull it back. What did this even mean? Frankly, I never found out because anytime I asked (which was many times) my managers were not able to put into words why being edgy was an area for improvement. Or at least they couldn't put it in a way that was politically correct enough for HR to give the green light." Jena describes reflecting back on what this feedback really meant. She later determined that "too edgy" meant not conforming—she just didn't fit in with the in-crowd, even though she did good work.

She later polled hundreds of women who had been told they were too (fill in the blank) at some point in their careers. The list included the following:

- Too Ambitious

- Too Intense

- Too Direct

- Too Feisty

- Too Focused

- Too Sexy

- Too Smiley

- Too Nice

- Too Quiet

- Too Loud

- Too Excited

- Too Strong

- Too Quirky

- Too Sincere

- Too Young

- Too Much

- Too Redhead (yes, this is real)

Jena then asked the women to translate what was "too" about themselves by viewing it as a unique strength. Interpretations included "a female founder who reported being called 'Too Much.' Her interpretation of 'Too Much' is her presence, energy, and appetite for life is all TOO intimidating." One of my own, *too quiet*, was reimagined as reflective. What's your "too"?

In a favorite episode of the *I Hate My Boss* podcast, the manager did not even try to make his reasons HR-appropriate when telling a female direct report that she was not up for promotion. He simply told her that she was not promoted "due to intangibles."[1] During her "interesting performance review that lasted for nearly two hours," this young woman was instructed to get more experience and become more assertive before she would be eligible for a promotion. She knew that in any of the company's other locations she would already be at a higher level based on her work quality and responsibilities. The fact that her leaders were looking for "intangibles" and wanted her to "command

---

1   https://www.stitcher.com/podcast/wondery/i-hate-my-boss/e/50774084

the room" led her to the realization that no woman had ever held that position. Maybe no woman ever will.

Her boss also admitted that men were promoted to "unsuitable or made-up positions" because they made a lot of noise about it. Host Liz Dolan has seen this situation more than once. "Intangibles, right there, red flag…be more assertive, second red flag, and the ultimate catch-22 for women. They tell you to be more assertive, and then the moment you are, they fire you." Basically, leadership wants you to command the room but without being commanding. This is a classic *double bind* for women. Sadly, it can be very challenging for women to get clear goals and measures so they can be held to those and not the so-called intangibles.

Making the Leap

Just one year after joining Redfin, in 2015 I made the leap. I left corporate work behind and started my own business, Reverb. Based in Seattle, we help fast-growing companies of all sizes foster a healthy culture, engage their employees, and develop their leaders. My company is growing faster than I had imagined, and I'm working harder than ever, but it's not an exhausting time in my life. In fact,

> *"I get to choose family and take care of my team, my clients, and myself."*

it's less stressful than anything I've done in the previous fifteen years.

When I started the business, my goals included taking my daughter to school, choosing whom I worked with and for, and having fun. I purposely work with clients in the Seattle area, so I don't have to travel. Having control over my schedule lets me work when I'm most productive, whether that means getting up at 5:00 a.m. to catch up when things are quiet or taking Friday afternoon off to drive my daughter to a climbing competition. I get to choose family *and* take care of my team, my clients, and myself. These are the terms and conditions I've always wanted. I just needed time and experience to get here.

I wrote this book because I know countless women who want and deserve the same, but they are unsure if it's truly possible.

HOW THIS BOOK CAME TO BE

In 2017, my client Jackie Haggerty at ExtraHop asked me to participate on a Ladies in Seattle Tech panel during a Women's Day celebration. Each of the speakers gave a five-minute lightning talk in response to the question "What career advice do you wish you were given years ago?" It was a diverse panel, and our answers revolved around the challenges each of us had personally navigated. While there were some commonalities, there were also stark differences based on our personalities, career paths, and the industries we'd chosen. Afterward, groups of women congregated around each of us. It was as if everyone in the audience had found someone they resonated with, someone who was telling *their* story. The sense of validation in the room was palpable, and I knew right then that telling women's stories is powerful!

To begin the book, I contacted thirteen successful, mission-driven women I knew and admired. My questions to them were about family, kindness, competition, money, and privilege. Their answers were not what I'd expected: They were more inspiring, eye-opening, and provocative than I could have ever imagined. These women oozed with authenticity and no-holds-barred honesty.

In nearly thirty hours of interviews, I heard in detail how these women—

- Pursued their goals without worrying if they'd fit in or not

- Were driven by collaboration rather than competition with others

- Were held back and championed by both women and men

- Became their own bosses to create better cultures

- Emerged as advocates for other women and underrepresented groups

Their experiences demonstrated how much we can learn from women's stories, and they were a timely reminder that so much change is still needed before women can truly be themselves.

Their stories also serve as a powerful confirmation to the rest of us that our own choices and actions matter. Each of us can effect positive change at work and in our own lives.

* * *

I also took the pulse of the younger generation, referred to throughout the book as Next Gen. My team talked to ten dynamic women, ages seventeen to thirty-three. They helped provide clarity on which issues are still a problem in the workplace, what they're doing about it, and what kind of support they need from their colleagues. These up-and-coming professional women made one thing clear—this book had to look at what's tough and include topics such as—

- The hierarchy of privilege in business

- The challenges of motherhood at work

- The unnecessary competition between women

- The realities of the #MeToo movement

It's Been Going on Forever

On a recent visit to New York City, my ninety-two-year-old grand-mother Beatrice told me about walking out on jobs twice back in the 1940s. While sitting at her desk as an accountant for a New York City retailer, she said the owner touched her from behind in an inappropriate way. She got up from her chair, walked out the door, and never went back. Later, in another job, again, a male boss went beyond what she described as the standard flirting that in her day any attractive, young woman expected at work. "There was pressure, and things got complicated." She acknowledged that not every woman could simply cut bait, because often a paycheck is too important to walk away from. But she was grateful she had the means to leave when she did.

Before exiting the corporate world, I had been questioning my choices, my strength, my tolerance, and my resiliency. I could see how feeling overworked and underappreciated had become status quo for many of my friends and colleagues. I thought: *How can others put up with this and I can't?* I saw being able to manage the pressure as a strength and juggling everything without dropping the ball as an achievement. *If others could handle it, why did my threshold keep getting lower? Why couldn't I hang in there and not let little things get under my skin?*

The truth is, if it weren't for my daughter's intervention, I might still be grappling with these questions and trying to make it work, just as women since my grandmother's time have done.

Becoming Better Advocates: No Turning Back

Today, with Time's Up, Black Lives Matter, #MeToo, and LGBTQIA+ empowerment, there's pressure to change the way we relate at work and to build healthy, inclusive cultures that are better for everyone. There's much that we, as women, managers, and leaders, are still trying to decipher. And now, men are filled with questions too, about their power, roles, and unconscious biases. There's a collective drive to become better advocates. How do we create modern workplaces where everyone can thrive? How can people with demands and interests outside of work grow their careers? What will it take for everyone to feel a sense of belonging? The women I spoke to offer us some remarkable ideas.

You'll notice, we don't wallow in anger or blame in this book. I subscribe to Ruth Bader Ginsburg's philosophy: "Fight for the things that you care about, but do it in a way that will lead others to join you." This is not "just another book about women's empowerment" or how to succeed in your career. This book is designed to help you reclaim your power, improve your situation, and become an advocate for yourself and others. #MeToo has opened the doors for conversation, education, and a new way of working together. There's no turning back. The thirteen women featured here will provide the bulk of the wisdom.

I've also included some experiences of my own. As a female business owner, I'm honored to have received recognition by being quoted in *The Wall Street Journal* and *Fast Company*. Recently I was added to the Forbes HR Council, and even crowned as a "Boss Tactician" by Seattle's own KUOW podcast, *Battle Tactics for Your Sexist Workplace*. These milestones gave me a shot in the arm when I needed them and let me know that I'm making a difference for my women colleagues. Being a leader takes resilience, tenacity, and the willingness to be both humble and bold. And there's always a learning edge that keeps me on my toes.

Until now, I hadn't examined the unique challenges for professional women of color. I saw us all as "women" in the same fight against the same stereotypes. My ignorance of their struggles

> *"Being a leader takes resilience, tenacity, and the willingness to be both humble and bold."*

as black, brown, and indigenous women meant I didn't know how to advocate for them effectively. I'm honored that several women of color shared their stories with me, so that I can share them with you. No matter your race or gender, as you read this book you might see how your own unrecognized privilege has opened doors for you that are not open to others. I'd like to invite you to embrace what you don't know and let it inform who you become. Challenge your privilege by creating a standard that is more inclusive and brings others along.

What You'll Need to Survive, Lead, and Thrive

We're going to dive into a rich combination of women's stories that are explained by societal context and backed by data. It's a lot to take in, and their experiences may be new to you. *Female Firebrands* invites you to take a realistic look at what it means to be a woman in the workplace, so you can do what you need to do to thrive. As you read, you will—

- Develop tools and techniques to stand up and speak up on behalf of yourself and others when it's both difficult and necessary

- Get better at recognizing "little indignities" you don't have to tolerate

- Learn what it means to be an informed, empowered advocate for women

- Increase awareness of your own blind spots and biases so you can learn from them

- Recognize the role of privilege at work and how it can be used for positive change

I've included a checklist at the end of each chapter about standing up for yourself, advocating for others, and influencing change in your organization—so you can put to use what you're learning. I've also included suggestions for male allies and advocates, as well as HR, Diversity, and other business leaders. People who want to bring these concepts into their organizations can find research, checklists, automated tools, and consulting services online at https://reverbpeople.com/femalefire-brands/.

One last thing: you will notice that certain words throughout the text are presented in italics. If you run across a word that's unfamiliar to you, we've got you covered in the glossary at the end of the book.

So, let's get started!

PART ONE

FACE-TO-FACE
WITH THE
FIREBRANDS

1

MAR BRETTMANN

EXECUTIVE DIRECTOR AT BEST: BUSINESSES ENDING SLAVERY AND TRAFFICKING

"Every day I work with people who are not privileged, who are not entitled. As a person who has incredible privilege because of my class, education and the color of my skin, I am just constantly trying to think of how I can use those privileges to help others who don't have them."

Mar Smith Brettmann, PhD, founded Businesses Ending Slavery and Trafficking (BEST). As a professor of philosophy, ethics, and religion for ten years at Fuller Theological Seminary, the University of the West Indies, and Whitworth University, she wrote and published articles about human rights, including "Jobs Must be Part of the Solution to Human Trafficking,"[2] "The Perfect Storm for Hotel Owners,"[3] and "Inhospitable to Human Trafficking."[4]

During her research, she became increasingly concerned about the brutal exploitation of children, women, and impoverished laborers that takes place through human trafficking. As the founder and executive director of BEST, Mar now educates business leaders and provides them with tools to implement socially responsible strategies that prevent human trafficking. Mar is the author of the book *Theories of Justice*. She has a BA in business and economics from Wheaton College and a PhD in theology and ethics from the University of St. Andrews in Scotland. Mar resides in Seattle with her family. She loves to explore the outdoors by foot, kayak, bike, surfboard, or snowboard.

---

2   "Jobs Must be Part of the Solution to Human Trafficking," *The Hill*, January 12, 2019.

3   Mar Brettmann, "The Perfect Storm for Hotel Owners," *Today's Hotelier*, November 2017.

4   Mar Brettmann, "Inhospitable to Human Trafficking," *Today's Hotelier*, December 2016.

WHAT MAKES MAR
A FEMALE FIREBRAND

Fighting Traffickers and Giving Survivors a Voice

As you might expect from someone who started an organization to prevent human trafficking in the United States, Mar is compassionate, collaborative, selfless, and driven. With a small team and a working board, Mar has single-handedly grown BEST into the only organization of its kind. BEST works with businesses, hotel owners' associations, and other nonprofits to achieve comprehensive change in the trafficking space.

Mar left academia when she realized that even as professors, women were not treated as equals by their male colleagues. Mar realized the way people treated her in academia led to unfounded self-doubt, so she turned to authors such as George Eliot, Sue Monk Kidd, and Simone de Beauvoir to help her make sense of her experience.

"Reading feminist thought and feminist theory helped me realize that it wasn't me who was doing anything wrong. When things weren't going right, I was always internalizing the belief that it was my fault; that I wasn't good enough. But the women around me, and the feminist thinkers I was reading, helped me to see what was happening more clearly." Mar knew she had a choice to make, and she opted to leave academia and make a future where she would be valued for who she was, while making a difference in the world. In 2012, she founded BEST.

BEST's mission includes working with businesses, corporations, and hotel owners' associations to create policies and training that reduce the incidence of trafficking in order to make the world safer for women and other marginalized groups. Businesses are key to preventing trafficking. Research shows that the peak time for buying sex online is 2:00 p.m.—in the middle of the workday. The highest percentages of men arrested for buying sex from underage girls are employed in the retail, transportation, manufacturing, IT, and construction industries.

BEST's online and in-person training for employers includes a list of websites for companies to block in order to stop their employees from buying sex online. BEST also offers resources to help companies create anti-trafficking policies. Most trafficking victims are "bought" in hotels, so BEST teaches hotel owners and employees that trafficking is not acceptable. Hotel employees learn how to identify and report trafficking, and staff are taught to implement specific best practices that prevent the sexual exploitation of children and women in hotels and motels.

Mar has the awareness and humility that allow her to work effectively with survivors of trafficking, who are predominantly women, and disproportionately women of color. While working in academia, Mar taught herself to speak up in order to be heard. "I spent so much time trying to find my voice. So, I want to have my voice all the time. And I want to speak my voice boldly all the time, because I spent so much time feeling like I had lost it; like it was being minimized by the people around me." When Mar goes into a situation with survivors, she quiets her voice. She makes room for theirs.

> *"I want to have my voice all the time. And I want to speak my voice boldly all the time."*

2

TERI CITTERMAN

EXECUTIVE PERFORMANCE COACH
AND AUTHOR OF
FROM THE CEO'S PERSPECTIVE

"I don't really care what other people are doing. I'm just going to be the best at what I do. I'm the first to say I don't belong; I'm an outlier. It's funny . . . sometimes, when we talk about authenticity, I think it's just the stupidest thing. I really do, because I don't understand how else you would be."

Teri Citterman coaches CEOs and senior executives who lead companies ranging from startups to Fortune 500s, including Alaska Airlines, CenturyLink, Lockheed Martin, Virginia Mason Medical Center, WeWork, Regence Healthcare, University of Washington Medicine, Bill & Melinda Gates Investments, and Microsoft. Her latest book, *From the CEO's Perspective*, provides a peek into the thinking of today's top CEOs. For twenty years, Teri has provided advice and thought leadership on internal and external communications and how to leverage power and influence. She is an award-winning writer, a regular contributor to *Forbes*, a sought-after speaker, and a thought cultivator for "The CEO's Perspective," a leadership forum. Teri's favorite places to explore are cemeteries because they hold the stories and history of a community. Her life's motto is "Who's going to stop me!"

WHAT MAKES TERI
A FEMALE FIREBRAND

An Authentic Outlier

I have a sneaking suspicion that lots of people want to be Teri when they grow up. Her intense, direct style makes her the perfect coach for CEOs. Teri hosts a CEO forum that's always sold out, bringing together the Pacific Northwest's most influential leaders with timely topics including purpose-driven leadership, building diverse companies, and the obligation of CEOs to speak up on social issues. By engaging senior leaders in conversations about *inclusion* and social justice, Teri encourages her audience to take on these issues in the workplace. Her panelists demonstrate both compassion and vulnerability—key leadership traits that many executives still hide behind a polished façade. The CEOs Teri brings on stage role-model what we need from the next generation of business leaders to create mission-driven organizations where people can safely bring their whole selves to work.

With no young children and as the stepmother to a teenage son, Teri has the freedom to be selfish with her time. Her favorite kind of relaxation includes reading books about leadership. Teri describes herself as "an outlier but not an outcast." She's fiercely independent and states unapologetically that her company and family are her first priorities. If she's going to take time away from what she loves most, it needs to be time well spent where she can make a difference. Unlike many women I meet, Teri has little difficulty saying no. In fact, she's made it a goal to check her generosity by trying to say yes more often when she's asked to help others. We can all learn from Teri's commitment to prioritize herself and her work without feeling guilty.

Teri has fought for fair pay by negotiating every job offer she ever received. If pay wasn't negotiable, she would ask for more vacation time. She intentionally negotiates after the so-called "best and final" offer and feels good about getting what she deserves. She's learned to fight for respect at work, having faced derogatory remarks from coworkers. "I'm pretty cavalier, because I've heard people talk about Jews, not knowing I'm Jewish. I remember someone saying, 'If there were any Jews in the room, I would know.' I didn't have the courage to say anything."

After that incident, Teri made sure she was prepared to speak up. When a coworker made a lewd remark, she told him, "I'm going to let you take that back. You have twenty seconds." Being ready to respond empowered Teri, and she wants to pass that on to younger women. When Teri mentors early career women, she makes sure they too are ready to respond to sexist remarks. It's an unfortunate reality, but Teri addresses this head-on so young women won't be caught off guard if they are hit on or disparaged at work.

When she realized that coaching CEOs was her passion, Teri had to overcome her own impostor syndrome in order to turn her passion into her life's work. She questioned herself, thinking, "Why would a CEO want to be coached by me? What qualifications do I have to coach a CEO?" She considered coaching leaders at other levels, but she cares deeply about the challenges that CEOs face, and knew she had the skills to make them more effective. "Doing anything else felt complicated, so I just had to own it. I just had to say, 'This is what I do,' and believe it. I had to figure out what my fear was and overcome that." As an introvert, making a bold statement like this felt incredibly risky. How did Teri overcome her fears? She started coaching CEOs—simple as that. She later wrote a book called *From the CEO's Perspective* to establish herself publicly as an expert in her field.

3

FRAN DUNAWAY

CEO/CO-FOUNDER, TOMBOYX

"I came out as a lesbian at the age of twenty-one. I was delighted, because I was like, 'Oh! That's what's wrong with me. I mean, that's what's right with me.' You know, you do things to look the way your mother from Mississippi wants you to look, or you do things to make a career change, or to strive for a particular accomplishment. That means you have to change how you look and how you present."

Fran Dunaway likes to call herself the accidental entrepreneur. In 2013, she had a great life as a partner in a media strategies firm with big budgets and lots of vacation time. That free time led her and her wife, Naomi Gonzalez, to start a side business—because they wanted some cool button-down shirts!

They picked the name TomboyX because they thought it was cute, and because the word "tomboy" opens the door to conversations about being whoever it is you want to be. When the name started to resonate with women and girls around the world, they knew they had an instant brand. Today, TomboyX has refocused solely into the underwear/loungewear market. Their message has hit home. Because people of all shapes and sizes want to unite behind a brand that stands for the values they share, TomboyX is thriving.

WHAT MAKES FRAN
A FEMALE FIREBRAND

Making People Comfortable in Their Own Skin

Fran is active nationwide in the *LGBTQIA+* community. Her company, TomboyX, which she started with wife Naomi Gonzalez, is an inspiring and innovative underwear brand that embraces gender fluidity through its myriad styles. I am inspired by Fran and Naomi's grit as two female founders who are unapologetically themselves. I love the ethos Fran has imbued into her company to own that you are cool however you are, and that you deserve to feel unapologetically good in your own skin, every day.

As a startup founder, Fran faced her share of challenges. Many founders struggle to make a living while getting a new business off the ground. When both partners are invested in the business, as Fran and Naomi are, things can get tricky. More than once she feared they wouldn't make it. They went without a salary for two years. At one point, another company launched in the Northwest with similar products and a significantly bigger marketing budget.

Fran and Naomi were getting multitudes of requests to make boxer briefs for women, and so they did some research and found that no one else was making those products. Rather than compete with the other company, they decided to step further into the white space of an unfulfilled need, thus finding the hero product around which to build a great brand.

Instead of getting angry, which is unproductive, Fran says they took the high road, and this became the impetus for their evolution into an underwear company. Fran is not only confident that TomboyX will win in this category, she believes strongly that brands emulate their founders. If that's the case, and I believe it is, then TomboyX has nothing to fear.

Fran describes what happened when she and Naomi first realized that TomboyX was resonating with a wide audience. "We saw an opportunity to address an unmet market of people who were so excited that there was finally a brand that saw them and recognized them. It became a responsibility." She goes on to talk about what the brand means to her and to society. "I think the TomboyX brand is on the pulse of a cultural change. It's not a trend; it's a new way of thinking and living and being in the world. A lot of that is around women's empowerment, but also societal norms around gender, and how much that's been hammered into us." Fran says, "It's just clothing, after all. Shouldn't you be comfortable?"

In January 2019, TomboyX won the Greater Seattle Business Association (GSBA) Business of the Year Award. (GSBA describes itself as the largest LGBTQ and allied chamber of commerce in North America.) "As the company's growth has ballooned over the past six years, taking in $5.4 million of revenue in 2017, its tenets of body-positivity and empowerment have remained steady."[5]

Once a put-down for girls who weren't considered feminine enough, I asked Fran what was behind their choice of names. "We chose TomboyX because we thought it was a cute name for a company and it was available to trademark. We both identified as tomboys when we were kids and feel like that spirit is still a big part of who we are. And yes, we wanted to reclaim it in a way that was ours." Here's their definition of "tomboy"[6]:

1. An energetic, sometimes boisterous girl.

2. An individual who dresses and sometimes behaves the way boys are expected to.

3. A girl or a woman or person who DGAF about definitions 1 and 2.

4. Someone who is utterly, completely, and unapologetically themselves; who is not afraid to stand up, stand out, be heard, be seen. On their terms.

5. A woman or a person who expresses and dresses themselves in a way that feels authentic to themselves without worrying about what other people might say.

6. A person who is damn okay with who they are.

7. Not a phase.

8. You?

9. Me.

---

5   https://thegsba.org/about-us/blog/gsba-blog/2019/01/24/meet-tomboyx-gsba's-2018-business-of-the-year

6   https://tomboyx.com/pages/about-us-1

4

LESLIE FEINZAIG

FOUNDER AND CEO,
FEMALE FOUNDERS ALLIANCE

"I don't have a medium setting of caring. I just don't. If I am going to be true to myself and continue to give my heart, soul, and time to a professional endeavor, then I'm going to do it for something that I care about—something that I truly, truly, truly care about."

L eslie Feinzaig is the founder and CEO of the Female Founders Alliance (FFA), a grassroots network of high-growth startup founders and CEOs dedicated to helping each other succeed. What started as an informal online group has grown more than ten times in just over a year, bringing together hundreds of female founders from across North America. In 2016, Leslie launched Venture Kits, kids' games that develop leadership skills through play. Her one-of-a-kind, inspirational concept quickly garnered critical acclaim and a feature on the *Today* show "Parents." Prior to Venture Kits and FFA, Leslie held product leadership roles in prominent tech companies including Julep, Big Fish Games, and Microsoft. Leslie was named to the *Puget Sound Business Journal's* 40 Under 40, *Seattle* magazine's Most Influential People, and *Forbes's* 100 Most Powerful Women from Central America and the Caribbean. Leslie has a BSc from the London School of Economics and an MBA from Harvard Business School. She was born and raised in San Jose, Costa Rica, and now lives in Seattle with her husband, their three-year-old daughter Dora and three-week-old daughter Ruth.

WHAT MAKES LESLIE A FEMALE FIREBRAND

Creating Access and Opportunity for Female Founders

When I first heard about a new organization that invests in the success of female-founded startups, I knew I had to meet the woman behind the Female Founders Alliance (FFA). I introduced myself to Leslie to learn more about her work, and since then I've been honored to coach Leslie and partner with her company. I immediately admired her independence, perseverance, and originality. Leslie describes herself this way: "I never felt like I belonged anywhere my whole life, so I just kind of gave up that dream early. I don't try to belong; it is what it is. I grew up a White girl in a Latin country. I grew up Jewish in a Catholic school and then I moved to the States and I'm like an immigrant Latina, I am a woman in a male-dominated industry . . . I've never belonged anywhere. I was a cheerleader who was a nerd. I was a nerd who was a cheerleader. So, no, I don't feel I've ever compromised who I am in order to belong 'cause I just don't belong and that's that."

Leslie is a staunch believer that there's room for plenty of women at the top. She asks, "Why would you not root for each other? Why would you not believe that there's room for all of us?" It was her own struggle to find a community of like-minded women that led her to create FFA, originally an online group where female founders could connect. "I have created a community where the belief that there's only room for one woman at the top is unacceptable."

Leslie is not only fiercely determined; she's driven by her mission to advance professional women. Leslie's celebration of women and their allies has shifted my own thinking about what it means to believe in women's *equity*, take action, and become a true champion for women. Her goal of advancing women's equity before her daughters Dora and Ruth enter the workplace makes her relentless in her work to find meaningful solutions.

Leslie turned 2.19%—the amount of venture funding that goes to female founders—into a mantra. With her leadership, FFA has been key to taking actions that effect real change. The organization gives women access to decision-makers and forges meaningful relationships through public speaking, media appearances, and investor introductions. FFA recognized from the beginning that women need much more than mentoring and advice to get the opportunities they deserve.

In 2018, Leslie launched the first ever Champion Awards—a sold-out event where 350 people came to show their support for female founders. In the midst of allegations that sparked the latest wave of the *#MeToo* movement, Leslie saw an opportunity to celebrate the good. She highlighted role models, allies, and *advocates* who are helping women rise.

Her work has been featured in *Fast Company*, *GeekWire*, and the *Seattle Times*. When she speaks and writes, Leslie herself communicates in a way that is both personal and vulnerable. In one of her blog posts,[7] she challenged anyone who doesn't think women can succeed, work as equals, and have an impact on society with her mantra #watchme. In March 2019, she released a blog post titled "I Am 33 Weeks Pregnant," accompanied by a photo of herself on stage with a microphone, visibly pregnant. "I acknowledged it from the get-go. Stopping short of calling out the 'elephant in the room'—because at 33 weeks that's more self-deprecating than even I'm willing to be—I told the audience: 'I bet you're not used to seeing a 33-week pregnant woman keynote at an event like this.' And they laughed. Because I was right."

---

7   https://femalefounders.org/i-am-33-weeks-pregnant/

5

CHERYL INGRAM

CEO AND FOUNDER,
DIVERSE CITY AND INCLUSOLOGY

"My primary goal is to always educate. Meet the person where they are and communicate so they can understand the message you want them to hear. Never hold back but think about how to phrase things so that the person you are talking to actually receives the message. My second goal is to make sure I am authentic and courageous—that I say what I need to say."

C heryl Ingram is the CEO and founder of Inclusology (a software company that is working to build the world's greatest benchmarks for *diversity,* equity, and inclusion [DEI]) and Diverse City LLC (a diversity and inclusion consulting firm working with organizations across the United States). Cheryl has been training and coaching in the area of multicultural studies for fifteen years. She has her Doctorate of Education with a specialization in multicultural studies, a Master of Arts in education, and her Bachelor of Arts in communication studies, all from New Mexico State University. She has been a professor of multicultural studies for eight years and currently teaches courses at Shoreline Community College in Shoreline, WA. Cheryl's many passions related to social justice and equity include serving on the board of directors for Unloop, a national technical training program that addresses recidivism in prisons throughout Washington State.

WHAT MAKES CHERYL
A FEMALE FIREBRAND

Diversity, Equity, and Inclusion Champion

Cheryl is a prominent diversity, equity, and inclusion (DEI) expert who guides leaders and teams through difficult yet necessary conversations about diversity and unconscious bias at work. Every time I talk to Cheryl, I learn something new. That's why in 2018 I asked Cheryl to join Reverb as a key partner and advisor. When she facilitated an Unconscious Bias session for our team, it was the most effective diversity training any of us had ever experienced. Her training led us through a self-reflection about who we trust and spend time with—by race, gender, ability, and sexual orientation. Most of us quickly realized that the people in our inner circle look a lot like us, and in order to have real diversity in our lives we need to be more intentional. Cheryl taught us about twelve types of unconscious bias, helping us recognize different ways that bias can show up and how deeply rooted it is.

Cheryl talks with candor about her challenges as a black woman, confronting the resistance that comes with her occupation. DEI work can be deeply personal, and often makes people feel uncomfortable and even threatened. Cheryl faces resistance even from her own clients. Some clients try to control how Cheryl talks about diversity, what information she shares with their teams, even what she can and can't say while working with them. After her first year as a consultant, she had a realization. "I'm the expert here. I know diversity. I've been doing this for a really long time. Why am I letting these people tell me what to do?"

Clients aren't always comfortable with Cheryl's honest, direct communication style. At times she has sensed fear and hesitation during contracting client meetings. One client even asked that they limit communications to email—no face-to-face contact. To her credit, Cheryl is now willing to walk away from business when she senses that the client is not ready to listen, be vulnerable, and participate in hard conversations. "I walked away from a really nice-sized contract because I could tell they weren't comfortable with me showing up as my authentic self. I have just gotten to a point where if I can sense in the interview process and the way that they're vetting me, if it doesn't seem like something beneficial long-term. No matter how much I want to serve the populations in those spaces. I've come to the realization that my mental sanity is more important. So, I've started to walk away."

Cheryl knows she has to be prepared—for the resistance, comments, and challenges she faces daily. "I work on training myself to navigate difficult conversations and hard moments. It's a shame that I have to practice for shit like that, but I do."

It's easy to imagine that these struggles would wear Cheryl down. It's a testament to her character and mission that Cheryl is clear about the value she brings to organizations, and the impact she can have. It's not always easy, but she has a technique to remind herself of her worth. "One of the things that was a huge growth area for me as a black woman and especially a black woman in professional spaces was unconsciously not realizing how much I didn't think I deserved certain things. It was like this deprogramming of myself to make myself believe like, 'You deserve to be here as much as anybody else. You're intelligent. You know your shit.'"

6

CHRISTY JOHNSON

CEO AND FOUNDER,
ARTEMIS CONNECTION

"There have been times where I've been asked to make sure I wear a certain dress and heels and have my hair a certain way, and then to make sure I sit next to certain men in meetings. I'm not going to do that again. That crossed a line for me."

C hristy has seven years of experience working in corporate strategy, including three and a half years at McKinsey & Co. Christy was previously an award-winning economics and mathematics teacher, recognized in 2005 by Junior Achievement as its National Teacher of the Year. She holds an MBA from Stanford's Graduate School of Business with a certificate in public management. She also has a master's in education from Stanford's School of Education. Her undergraduate degree is in economics from Western Washington University.

Christy is an entrepreneur and educator. She is currently running her third startup, Artemis Connection, whose mission is to partner with organizations to build amazing strategies that are easy to execute and have a positive impact on both their employees and their external communities. Artemis also hosts the annual ASCEND Leadership Summit, a full-day event dedicated to discussing inclusion, diversity, equity, and access in American workplaces. In addition, Christy facilitates a course on designing organizations for creativity and innovation at the Stanford Graduate School of Business. She believes people are an organization's most important asset and that by having a diverse workforce, organizations will generate the most innovative solutions.

Christy resides in Mukilteo, Washington, with her husband, Kyle Johnson, her daughter, and twin boys.

WHAT MAKES CHRISTY A FEMALE FIREBRAND

Strategist, Innovator, Entrepreneur

I met Christy when we collaborated on an online compilation of resources for women in technology. I quickly came to admire her passion and data-driven approach to gender equality. Christy has taken the initiative to advance gender and racial equality through her work at Artemis, and by hosting a monthly Pacific NW Diversity Meetup, where local leaders, including representatives from Washington State Governor Jay Inslee's office, work together on solutions for some of the region's toughest DEI issues. Noting the absence of gender equality data in startup companies, Christy launched a survey in 2017 providing this information for the first time ever in Seattle.

Christy always knew she wanted to be a mom. Her kids bring her more joy than she ever could have imagined, and she treasures every moment with them, even the "temper-tantruming times." It's not easy to run a business, travel to client meetings, and be there for your family, but Christy has figured out which trade-offs make it work for her.

Christy is an entrepreneur at heart and loves teaching. While she's aware of her limits as one individual, she believes that "If I can inspire others to be inclusive, values-driven, strategic, and data-driven leaders who want to make the world a better place, then I'll feel good about my life."

This all started when she was teaching public high school and brought economics into her classroom curriculum. Christy says, "I also wove entrepreneurship into my math courses, since it engaged students so much more than the standard textbooks." Christy enjoys getting to know all the students she's met through teaching high school, facilitating courses at Stanford, and designing then launching a course for the University of Washington.

Christy marvels at the effort that goes into teaching when it's done well and is customized to meet students' needs. "It's a ton of work to design a course, meet the students, learn about them collectively and individually, and curate a learning experience that will build mastery of skills. I still have so much respect for teachers, principals, and superintendents in public schools."

As an entrepreneur, Christy enjoys creating good-paying jobs for people who are underemployed or out of the labor market. This includes people who have faced bias or discrimination, who live outside of urban areas, and those who need flexibility because they are caring for children or aging parents.

7

ERIN JONES

EDUCATION CHAMPION,
SOCIAL JUSTICE ADVOCATE,
EDUCATOR, AND PUBLIC SPEAKER

"I am Erin Jones. I am black, and I am white. I'm European, and I'm American. I'm a jock, and I'm an academic. I am kind of nerdy, but I'm also a baller. I fill up spaces, and I just own that. I have this giant Afro. I just am. I just am. And if you have a problem with it, that's your problem; it's not mine. I say it like it is."

Erin Jones has been an educator for twenty-five years and is a former teacher, school district director, and assistant state superintendent for the state of Washington. Erin ran for Washington State superintendent in 2016 because she believed we needed someone with long and effective experience in public education to be a voice for both students and educators. She was the first black woman in Washington to run for statewide office and lost that race by 1%. She leverages the platform created through her candidacy to inspire students and educators, and to provide training for stakeholder groups on how to employ equitable practices to better serve entire communities. Erin was raised as an expatriate in the Netherlands and speaks four languages. She and her husband of twenty-four years have three adult children.

WHAT MAKES ERIN
A FEMALE FIREBRAND

Lifelong Educator and Equity Advocate

I love it when colleagues—and men, in particular—send an introduction that says, "You two women must meet." That's what happened when our mutual friend, Steve Matly of SM Diversity, introduced us. Erin not only told me about her work in education, she shared the story of her childhood. When Erin was young, the white parents who adopted her left the United States and moved their family to the Netherlands. They raised Erin there from ages five through eighteen in order to avoid the racism they experienced in the United States. For example, on more than one occasion, they were refused a table at restaurants because they were a mixed-race family.

Although her childhood dream was to serve at the UN World Court as either an interpreter or a lawyer, Erin realized early in her college career that her talents would be best used as an educator. Over the past twenty-five years, Erin has used her skills as an educator working as a volunteer, a substitute, a teacher, and an instructional coach. She has worked in white and black communities, and in some of the most diverse communities in the nation. Today Erin is a keynote speaker, and an educational consultant who specializes in leading equity workshops for schools, nonprofits, government agencies, boards, and churches.

Erin has intentionally spent her career working in some of the poorest communities in the country. She has watched teachers who have limited resources themselves give and give to kids who have nothing. Watching how people with very little come together to support their own communities, Erin believes in kindness because she's seen it firsthand. She describes how her students in North Philly found ways to help each other. "Most of my kids had no running water or electricity. But they shared everything they had with each other. Somehow kids never went without, because they would figure out if someone needed clothes or food. These kids would share with each other like I've never seen in some of the loftier communities where I've lived."

As if a shortage of resources did not create enough of a challenge, Erin suffered at the hands of a boss who seemed bent on putting her down. He made it his mission, after she won a national award, to remind her she was no better than anybody else. But Erin is resilient, and cares deeply about the students she serves. "I decided that I will not allow him to define me. I will not allow him to tell me what I can and cannot do. I work for the children of our state, and no matter what he says, I will continue to do amazing work. I do not work for him." Every day, she reminded herself that her purpose was helping kids.

Painful as it was, that incident also taught Erin an important lesson: there is plenty of room for greatness. She does not believe in what she calls a deficit mentality, that you have to take anyone else down a peg if you're going to succeed. "We can't afford to destroy other people when they do great work. When someone is celebrated, we should all celebrate with them. There's enough celebration to go around."

In 2018, Erin spoke to and inspired 150,000 kids. She's doing the work she believes in most and is thriving as her own boss. "The beauty of being my own boss right now is, I can say it like it is, like I see it. I don't answer to anybody but myself, and it's the most beautiful space for me to be in."

8

HEATHER LEWIS

GOVERNMENT AFFAIRS MANAGER, ROVER.COM

"Sometimes on the weekend my daughter Amala comes to the office with me. She's very comfortable here. She loves to take snacks and feed the dogs, and she has a little standing desk that our CEO made for her. Her understanding of the kind of work women can do is being shaped by what I do. And I feel responsible for that."

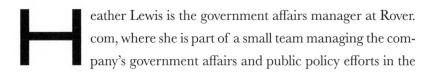

eather Lewis is the government affairs manager at Rover.com, where she is part of a small team managing the company's government affairs and public policy efforts in the

United States, Canada, the UK, and eight European countries. Prior to this, she served as the Director of the Fast Pitch program at Social Venture Partners and advised the University of Washington leadership team on technology and innovation policy and commercialization strategy. Heather has served as a member of several nonprofit, for-profit, and government boards, including the Western Governors University Board of Advisors. She holds a bachelor's degree from the University of British Columbia, an MPA in science and technology policy, and certificates in technology entrepreneurship and technology law and public policy from the University of Washington business and law schools. She is currently working on her MBA from the University of Illinois at Urbana-Champaign.

WHAT MAKES HEATHER A FEMALE FIREBRAND

Civic and Community Leader

When I met Heather in 2016, she led a program called SVP Fast Pitch Seattle, a competition where social impact companies receive coaching and mentoring and then pitch their ideas to win money and services to help sustain their companies. While volunteering as a coach for the innovators, I was impressed by Heather's presence, composure, and ability to facilitate and drive decisions with a group of senior people. This type of work is often compared to "herding cats." Heather was flawless in her ability to drive consensus. She's a passionate parent, civic expert, and lifelong learner. Her values come through in everything she does. One secret to Heather's success may be that she completes a personal strategic plan at a getaway once a year with a close friend. I don't know many people who make that kind of investment in themselves.

As someone who gets energized by being around confident women, Heather seeks out places where women thrive. "I find that I am most effective in environments where there are high-performing women. So, I tend to seek them out because I want to get better, but also because I love being around other women who are doing great things." She makes it a point to create opportunities for younger women too, coaching and mentoring women who are looking for feedback to help them grow.

Heather says, "Overall, I suppose what I am most proud of (professionally speaking) is that I'm building a set of skills and experiences that can add value to those around me. My parents made it clear that we had an obligation to those around us, a 'responsibility to be excellent.' My dad was an elementary school principal in a school with many needs. This brought home the fact that poverty and reduced opportunities was a local/national problem as well as a global one."

As a manager, Heather works hard to role model authenticity and vulnerability. She is a big believer that it's kind to give constructive feedback. While feedback can sting in the moment, Heather knows if she isn't receptive she might not get it again. She often asks her team what she can do better. She works to normalize the idea that it's OK to be critical, in order to create the feedback *culture* she's striving for.

In addition to her work, Heather is always thinking about what kind of example she wants to set for Amala. Heather says, "I also want to make it clear to my daughter that she can be whomever she wants to be and aspire to any profession. That starts with creating an expectation that people with her background and people (especially women) with black and brown skin 'look like' engineers, CEOs, doctors, government leaders, etc. Women of all backgrounds belong everywhere important decisions are being made."

How does she do it all? As an introvert, Heather knows that she needs time alone to refuel. It was something she became increasingly aware of after her daughter was born. Now she's intentional about making trade-offs to protect her down time—making sure she gets the time she needs to sit alone or do her own thing. This way, Heather takes care of herself and avoids the risk of burnout.

9

EMILY PARKHURST

PUBLISHER AND MARKET PRESIDENT,
PUGET SOUND BUSINESS JOURNAL

"Authenticity is a must, both in my industry and as a manager of people. If you're not authentic with your team, they know it immediately. Being inauthentic is one of the number-one causes of management conflict in the workplace. Another problem is a lack of transparency, and I think those two things go hand in hand."

Emily Parkhurst is market president and publisher of the *Puget Sound Business Journal (PSBJ)*. She joined the *PSBJ* in 2012 and served as a technology reporter, managing editor, and editor-in-chief (the first woman to ever hold this position) prior to being named publisher in October 2018. Before 2012, Emily was an education and government reporter in her home state of Maine.

Emily is a national award-winning journalist. The *PSBJ* won the Society of Professional Journalists Sigma Delta Chi award for public service journalism in 2018 for its "Price of Homelessness" cover story, and the 2018 Society for Advancing Business Editing and Writing (SABEW) award for its multifaceted real estate reporting. Her series of stories on the restraint of schoolchildren in Maine won the Sigma Delta Chi award for investigative reporting in 2010. She holds a master's degree in creative writing from the Vermont College of Fine Arts, and an undergraduate degree in classical music performance from the University of Southern Maine.

WHAT MAKES EMILY A FEMALE FIREBRAND

Advocate for Women in Journalism

I met Emily for the first time at a Women in Technology event in 2017—the same one that prompted me to write this book. When five of us gathered to give five-minute "lightning talks" answering the question "What's the career advice you never got?" Emily confidently and unapologetically discussed being told repeatedly as a young woman to "tone it down" and soften her approach. Thank goodness she wholeheartedly rejected that advice because it made her a passionate, vocal, and outspoken role model for female journalists and other professional women.

If you met Emily today, you would never guess that as a little girl, she was painfully shy. Her shyness lasted until middle school, when she got over it. "I would sit in the back of the class, and I barely spoke up. I was nervous around the other kids, and teachers would tell me 'Emily, you should speak up more.'"

Emily felt nervous around her peers, but as she got older, she decided that was just silly. Not many people can make such a dramatic change by choice alone, but Emily did. She made a full 180-degree turn and has been forthright and outgoing ever since. Today, Emily makes it a point to participate in meetings. She realized that a meeting should not close without her speaking. She figured that out even before reading Sheryl Sandberg's book *Lean In*.

Emily knew that "If you don't speak up, you're invisible." Speaking out has also gotten her into hot water when she's felt passionate about controversial issues. "I have absolutely been outspoken in ways that have gotten me into trouble, and it has not been lost on me that in some cases men expressing these same thoughts and emotions might be perceived very differently. Because I'm a woman, I was perceived as overly aggressive. I know that I'm described that way, while a man in my position would be described as assertive."

Years ago, at a previous job, Emily worked with a male colleague who was making another member of the team uncomfortable. "There was this whisper network that we hear about so much now. Rather than address his behavior, people just said to make sure you're not alone with this guy after-hours. Women were told to just avoid him."

This man was sending inappropriate text messages to a young, female employee. When the young woman confided in her, Emily jumped into action, saying, "OK, we have to report this. This is incredibly important. I know you feel uncomfortable about this, so I'll go with you, and do whatever you need. But people have been whispering about this guy for a while, and now there's physical evidence in the form of text messages."

She did report the incident, and ultimately that man was fired. Without Emily, women might still just be avoiding and tolerating him. The experience of advocating for her young colleague informed the way Emily has handled similar situations, especially as a manager who feels a deep sense of responsibility for her team.

10

TET SALVA

FOUNDER, MOMWARRIOR[2]

"There is a Hawaiian proverb that says: 'It is through the way you serve others that your greatness will be felt.' If your intention is pure, everything else will follow. Yes, there will be challenges; but if you stay grounded in your truth and stick to your values, I believe things will fall into place. And it is in this place where you can better serve others; the universe, in turn, will reward you with fulfillment and compassion."

Tet Salva is the Founder of MomWarrior™ and a mother to four young daughters. MomWarrior is an online platform designed to support the advancement of women, specifically mothers, in the workplace. MomWarrior is the premier playbook for the modern mom. Tet is also a fierce advocate for immigrants and women of color, and often writes and speaks about the challenges they face. Her career took her on a journey from technology to retail, until she became an organizational transformation and change leader working with several Fortune 500 companies. Tet moved to the United States from the Philippines with no more than twenty dollars in her pocket, a lot of gumption, and an immense amount of faith. She graduated magna cum laude from Menlo College and continues to pursue learning at Stanford University.

WHAT MAKES TET
A FEMALE FIREBRAND

Connecting Purpose at Work
and at Home for Working Mothers

As part of her MomWarrior research on Parenthood and Purpose, Tet and her team interviewed more than 100 working moms and dads across the United States. They found that after becoming parents, 97% of participants gained a deeper sense of purpose, a whopping 99% wanted to create a more positive impact within their community at work, and 93% had a strong desire to seek personal growth.

An important and perhaps surprising finding was that working mothers appear to perform *even better* after having children. Motherhood ignited their purpose, giving their lives deeper meaning and a fresh perspective. Motherhood helped hone skills and enhance professional abilities that are not only relevant, but necessary to succeed in the modern workplace: resilience, emotional intelligence, efficiency, empathy, the ability to look at the long-term impacts of actions, and increased motivation—just to name a few.

This, she found, is the fire that women are now using to speak their minds and spearhead change within their communities and organizations. Tet says, "I find innovation incredibly sexy. And I thrive on building community and authentic connection. We all play multiple roles: mother, partner, daughter, sister, career professional, and so much more. We need to shift the paradigm to create the culture and infrastructure so our daughters and sons can go after their aspirations. I am working toward normalizing caregiving. And above all, my hope is that we get to the place of no guilt and bias for being human."

As an entrepreneur, Tet experimented quite a bit but eventually circled back to her original mission: to break down silos and barriers and *amplify* the voices of women—and men—who are trying to change the future of work. Tet is drawn to pursue the advancement of women—specifically those who are mothers, immigrants, and/or women of color. She realized that she had no desire to compete with others who were trying to solve the same problems. She would rather become the aggregator—the hub—than compete. Her mission is too important to go it alone.

More than once, Tet has had difficult encounters with senior women at work. Those experiences solidified her desire to support the women around her. "I have found that we, women, can be our own biggest nemesis. I don't want to be like that. I want to help women, because when we help each other, that's how we progress." Even though her rejection of the status quo went against her upbringing in a very conservative household, Tet knew she'd found her calling.

She still remembers her mom telling her, "Just follow what your teachers say. Just say yes and do what you are told." But Tet has never been comfortable with that approach. She has always tried to find a different, unconventional way of doing things. She's motivated today to do better for her four young daughters. "If we are going to tell our daughters they can be anything they want to become, then we better get our sh*t together."

11

MALA SINGH

CHIEF PEOPLE OFFICER, ELECTRONIC ARTS

"When I was young, as a woman of color who comes from a very unique and different background, I never felt like I could be truly authentic to what my background and upbringing was. For me, that's authenticity. It is about letting your story be told and having the power of voice to be able to share what you really feel, and what you really think and do, in a way that's unapologetic."

Mala Singh serves as chief people officer for Electronic Arts (EA), where she develops talent and cultivates the company's culture. In this role, Mala oversees Human Resources, Talent Acquisition, Workplaces, and Employee Services. Prior to that, she was chief people officer at a startup called Minted, where she helped shape the culture and expand the creative and technical teams during a high-growth period. Mala's early career was in Human Resources in Asia, Europe, and North America. She's spent eight years in various HR leadership roles at EA. Mala lives in the Bay Area with her family.

WHAT MAKES MALA
A FEMALE FIREBRAND

Advancing Inclusion and Belonging in Gaming

Mala balances a challenging role as chief people officer for Electronic Arts, a public company, while being a mother to three amazing kids and maintaining a loving relationship with her husband Darrin, who's a stay-at-home dad. Through her work at EA, Mala is transforming the people function and engaging her company and CEO in candid conversations about inclusion in an industry not always known for gender parity.[8]

As a young woman, Mala struggled to embrace her cultural background. "I present Indian female, so people ascribe all sorts of things. I can't tell you how many times I'm mistaken for having come from India, which is obvious. I have the looks, I have the name, but my culture is so different." Growing up in Guyana followed by what she

---

8   https://www.theguardian.com/technology/2017/mar/15/video-game-industry-diversity-problem-women-non-white-people

describes as "the classic immigrant life and situation" after moving to the United States, it's only in the last ten years that Mala has felt comfortable talking about her background and telling her story.

Fast-forward to today: she now has a platform to make change happen, with 9,000 EA employees, and even with their customers. Mala explains: "Through the games we make, we can help change the world through the stories we tell and the experiences we provide." When she witnesses behavior or hears comments that are an affront to the company's values, she calls it out. That means oftentimes, Mala is having some of the hardest conversations that others aren't willing to have.

After seeing award-winning actor and producer Viola Davis tell her origin story, Mala and her colleague, another senior woman executive, thought differently about a career talk they were preparing for EA employees. They asked themselves, "What if we owned our story? Instead of doing the usual 'here's how you can advance your career' talk, what if instead we talk about where we came from and how we grew up and the experiences we've had that shaped who we are?"

"We got up in front of an audience of about 400 people, including the CEO. My colleague and I sat on stage with a facilitator and told very intimate stories about how we grew up and the experiences we had, how we came into our own as women. We both had really tough childhoods and difficult circumstances. We laid it all out there, and we were not prepared for the impact that had on the group. People were inspired, and they could relate.

"I talked about growing up in a traditional situation, the expectations my parents had of me, and how I had to push against those and risk losing my parents in the process because it was the right thing to do. I couldn't bear to live the life I saw my mother have, which was subservient to the men in her life, denied education, and denied opportunity . . . relegated to only being a mother and not even celebrated for that. I thought, 'I'm not going to live that life.'"

A young man in the audience raised his hand and asked, "What advice do you have for me for how I can talk to my parents about the fact that I don't want to do this career they want, and I don't want to marry a girl, and I don't want to deal with all these things?" Mala observed, "This young Asian man stood up in an audience of 400 people and asked that question. The fact that by being that authentic and telling our true story we could actually connect that deeply with so many people was amazing."

It won't surprise you that Mala's motto is "When presented with the obvious, choose the different."

12

KIERAN SNYDER

CEO, TEXTIO

"My daughter loves school. She loves math. But she came home one day asserting that she was the 'math girl' in school. I was like, 'What does that mean?' Early in a girl's life, there's a paradigm of belief that there's only room for one girl. Her self-perception is already that she's competing for one slot."

K ieran is the CEO and co-founder of Textio, the augmented writing platform she founded with her husband that raised more than twenty million dollars. What is augmented writing? It tells you in advance how people will respond to what you say, giving you the power to see the future that your words will create. For instance, as you are writing a recruiting email in Textio Hire, the platform works with you to meld your ideas into language that will get a response from a diverse and relevant set of people. Textio's customers include companies like McDonald's and Johnson & Johnson. Prior to founding Textio, Kieran held product leadership roles at Microsoft and Amazon. Kieran has a PhD in linguistics from the University of Pennsylvania. Her work has appeared in *Fortune, Re/code, Slate,* and *The Washington Post.* Her articles include "The Abrasiveness Trap: High-Achieving Men and Women Are Described Differently in Reviews"[9] and "The Resume Gap: Are Different Gender Styles Contributing to Tech's Dismal Diversity?"[10]

WHAT MAKES KIERAN A FEMALE FIREBRAND

Aggressively Vigilant, Subversive Feminist

While there are challenges to being a founder and CEO, including the fact that it can be isolating and at times lonely, Kieran considers herself fortunate. "For all of the difficulty, I love my job. I wouldn't trade it for any job. My hardest days in this job are way better and more fulfilling than my best days at any other job I've had in the past. It really

---

9   http://fortune.com/2014/08/26/performance-review-gender-bias/

10   http://fortune.com/author/kieran-snyder/

is a privilege to get to do this. I think when leaders lose sight of that, they lose empathy with everybody around them. That can be really destabilizing for an organization. I am an incredibly lucky person to be able to be doing what I'm doing."

Kieran is thrilled by the kindness she's seen among women in the startup community. "I have experienced nothing but kindness and partnership from other women who found companies. I like to think I've given that back." And she certainly has, for instance putting extra time and energy into reviewing pitch decks from other female founders to increase their chances of raising venture money.

Working in large companies before founding her own, Kieran has had what she describes as common experiences, facing pregnancy discrimination and other types of sexist behavior. "I was told in a performance review that being pregnant was the reason I wasn't getting promoted. That's illegal. That sucks. That's not OK. I took my fantastic performance review. I thanked my manager, and I left the room. I didn't speak up."

Following her maternity leave, Kieran began to watch out for her women colleagues to make sure the same thing didn't happen to them. In her words, she became "aggressively vigilant."

Even as a CEO, Kieran is not immune to sexist remarks. She recalls a time when she was fund-raising and there was an investor who really wanted to invest in her company. He took her and Jensen (her husband/co-founder) out to lunch. He proceeded to tell a story about how he got into *venture capital*, saying, "Well, you know what it's like in venture. It's a bunch of geeky repressed guys holed up in their offices and their hot assistants tripping around on high heels." Kieran was appalled. This was coming from someone who wanted to invest in their company, who had proclaimed that he was interested in investing in more women-led companies. There was no question that they would turn him down. She reflects, "Is it shocking? Any time it happens you're like, did that really just come out of your mouth? But shocking? I don't know if it's shocking. It's just so common."

In addition to being a founder, CEO, mom of three girls, and basketball coach, Kieran describes herself as a subversive feminist. "A big subversive feminist thing I work hard at every single day is raising three girls in elementary school to be subversive feminists. They are going to grow up to achieve whatever they want, even if it is taking over the world." Kieran's other goal? "I continue to feel like the most subversively feminist thing I could possibly do is to turn Textio into a really big success."

13

RUCHIKA TULSHYAN

FOUNDER, CANDOUR, AND AUTHOR OF
THE DIVERSITY ADVANTAGE

"It's hard when your culture is very strongly stereotyped against you, and you need to play that down in the workplace. For instance, people will ask, 'Oh, did you have an arranged marriage?' I feel uncomfortable answering that because if I say yes (which is true, and I've written about it), then it's very easy to be typecast and stereotyped as someone who is traditional and not very ambitious. People will assume that I must be the primary caregiver and the submissive one at home."

Ruchika Tulshyan is founder of Candour, a firm focused on diversity and inclusion strategy and communications. As the author of *The Diversity Advantage: Fixing Gender Inequality in the Workplace*, Ruchika's mission is to foster honest conversations about barriers to equity at work. She is an award-winning journalist, whose work has been published in *Harvard Business Review* and *Forbes*. Her articles include "How Managers Can Make Casual Networking Events More Inclusive,"[11] and "Seattle-Area Women of Color Share How They Navigate the Workplace."[12] She was named 2019 Distinguished Professional-in-Residence for Seattle University's Communication Department. Ruchika is also co-chair of the Seattle Women's Commission and holds degrees from Columbia University and the London School of Economics. She is a Singaporean food-loving feminist who has worked in four countries.

WHAT MAKES RUCHIKA
A FEMALE FIREBRAND

Diversity and Inclusion Strategist and Award-Winning Journalist

Ruchika and I met when she spoke at an HR conference about her book, *The Diversity Advantage*. She writes for publications such as *Harvard Business Review* and *The Seattle Times*, and her articles on diversity, equity, and inclusion in the workplace are both informative and inspirational. Ruchika received the inaugural "2016 Women in Business

---

11 https://hbr.org/2018/10/how-managers-can-make-casual-networking-events-more-inclusive

12 https://www.seattletimes.com/pacific-nw-magazine/women-of-color-in-the-workplace/

and Leadership" award from the Seattle Metropolitan Chamber of Commerce for her work on advancing gender equality.

As a Singaporean immigrant and professor at Seattle University, Ruchika feels a unique pressure because she is always in the spotlight. "I know my students are watching me closely. Especially my students of color are watching the way that I present, the way that I speak, the way that I dress, and they're taking notes." She says the same is true as women move into senior leadership roles—other women are watching and getting inspired, but that means your behavior is under constant scrutiny. "It is exhausting to keep feeling like you better put away parts of your personality because not only do you not want to let your own self down, but you certainly don't want to let down the people who are looking up to you."

Ruchika highlights issues that don't always get attention, like the *double bind* faced by women in tech, where standard attire is jeans and a hoodie—for guys. What's wrong with that? Nothing, but consider the questions Ruchika poses in her article "Navigating Seattle's Hoodie-and-Jeans Work Culture as a Woman,"[13] including "Would we accept Facebook's COO Sheryl Sandberg if she wore the hoodies favored by her boss, Mark Zuckerberg?" Many professional women still feel pressure to dress the part, more so than their male counterparts.

Ruchika is a champion for women of color, using her platform to explore how they can find and use their voices, not only to speak up—but to get heard. For instance, Ruchika talked about *office housework* on one of my favorite podcasts—*Harvard Business Review*'s *Women at Work*. Office housework includes washing coffee mugs, ordering lunch, and planning parties for the team. There's nothing inherently wrong with these tasks, and it's good to pitch in. It's just that women get asked to

---

13   https://www.seattletimes.com/explore/careers/how-women-can-navigate-casual-workplace-dress-codes-in-seattle/

do them more often than men, and women of color get asked even more often than white women.

One shocking example? A nonprofit CEO who was asked to serve coffee to her own board. " . . . she was the first-ever Latina woman, first-ever woman of color, to lead one of the nonprofit organizations . . . she said, in the first board meeting that she ever had, she walked in, and the largely white male–dominated board asked her to serve coffee, knowing full well that she was CEO." Thank goodness she refused.[14] Ruchika gives practical advice we can all follow, on how to refuse such requests while still making it clear that you're a team player.

14   https://hbr.org/podcast/2018/09/lets-do-less-dead-end-work

PART TWO

FIREBRANDS GO FACE-TO-FACE WITH THE ISSUES

PRIVILEGE IN THE WORKPLACE

"When privilege is leveraged to expand opportunity for others, it is not a source of shame, but an ingredient to promote equity, increase creativity, and invite innovation. It's even the key to building community."

—Aiko Bethea

I can address the disadvantages I face as a white woman. When I hear about oppression of black and brown people, I have empathy, but I lack perspective. This is why I asked my friend and colleague, Aiko Bethea, head of diversity and inclusion at the Fred Hutchinson Cancer Research Center, to collaborate on this chapter with me. I believe this is a responsible way to examine the critical questions of race that were raised during my interviews and research for this book.

What Is Privilege?

My goal in this chapter is to help women define privilege and learn how it holds them back in business, whether intentionally or not. And when I talk about women, I'm referring to all women—black, brown, white, straight, gay, trans . . . I'll also mention *underrepresented minorities* (URMs), defined here as those who are most commonly underrepresented in high-tech organizations and Seattle-area startups, since those are the places where most of these stories take place. For the purpose of this section, URMs include people with disabilities, and racial and ethnic groups—blacks, Hispanics, American Indians, Alaska Natives, Pacific Islanders, Native Hawaiians, and those of two or more races.

All of us fall into different groups of *privilege* and *oppression*. Then there's *intersectionality*, which refers to the overlap of various social identities—race, gender, sexuality, class, ability, and so on. Because no one fits neatly into just one box, these conversations about privilege are situational and highly complex. Regardless of what privileges you do or don't have, my goal is that you will learn something new about how to recognize and respond to privilege when it's used to oppress, versus privilege when it's used responsibly. We'll end with suggestions for asserting yourself when someone else's privilege impedes your progress or interferes with your well-being.

This is not about judging yourself based on what privileges you have or feeling guilty. Having privileges doesn't mean you're arrogant, entitled, or have done something wrong. What matters is being aware of your privilege and recognizing how unmitigated privilege contributes to holding others back. I firmly believe those with privilege have a responsibility to recognize the advantages it provides and to use it not only for their own good, but also to boost and join forces with others who don't share the same privileges.

RUCHIKA TULSHYAN SAYS:
"If you have to think about privilege and wonder what it is, you already have it. You're a person with privilege if you've never had to worry about—

- being safe walking down the road being stopped at an airport or pulled over by a cop

- what other people think of your English

- people making fun of the food in your lunchbox

- being teased because of your family, culture, or customs."

Do a Privilege Check

HuffPost describes what it means to conduct a "privilege check" to help you understand and recognize various types of privilege:

- If I suggested that black people were over-reacting about Trayvon Martin, I might be told to check my (racial) privilege.

- If I said that gay people should stop complaining about marriage rights because they are free to love each other and that's all they need, I might be told to check my (hetero) privilege.

- If I suggested that my kid's school should stop sending home paper assignments and just let the kids do their homework from their own iPads, I might be told to check my (economic) privilege.[15]

---

15 Kristen Howerton, "White Privilege Doesn't Mean What You Think It Means" (blog), May 13, 2014, https://www.huffingtonpost.com/kristen-howerton/white-privilege-doesnt-me_b_5296914.html.

Why Does Privilege Matter?

A recent study shows that women at S&P 500 companies represent only 5% of CEOs. Gender disparity occurs in executive boardrooms, too, where women make up 16% of board members among the S&P 1500.[16] According to a *New York Times* analysis, there are almost as many CEOs named John in Fortune 500 companies as there are female CEOs in that category.[17] Can you believe that? "This is despite the fact that women make up 50.8% of the US population and 57% of college graduates, while Johns make up only 3.3% of those groups."[18]

Pause for a moment and close your eyes. Picture someone you know who has strong executive presence, who's maybe even a bit presidential in stature. Go ahead. Keep your eyes closed. Do you see a tall, fit, white man wearing a dark suit? By default, most Americans define leadership using stereotypically white, male attributes. That's because sports, government, and workplaces in our country were built by and for white men. This imbalance means all women and others in marginalized groups do not have equal power. Knowing this offers a tiny glimpse into the fraught and complicated path of the female professional.

Women joined the white-collar workforce in the 1860s, performing clerical roles. "It made sense that when women first entered the workplace, wearing a suit was a way to assert that they belonged and fit in with their male colleagues."[19] Women naturally emulated men's "business-like" dress and demeanor. Eventually those attempts

---

16   "Women CEOs of the S&P 500," *Catalyst*, October 3, 2018, https://www.catalyst.org/knowledge/women-ceos-sp-500.

17   "The Top Jobs Where Women Are Outnumbered by Men Named John," *New York Times*, April 24, 2018, https://www.nytimes.com/interactive/2018/04/24/upshot/women-and-men-named-john.html.

18   https://observer.com/2018/04/diversity-women-in-the-workplace-john/

19   https://www.fastcompany.com/40574667/from-armor-to-icon-the-enduring-appeal-of-the-power-suit

to assimilate were deemed "too masculine," causing a swing of the pendulum to appearance and behaviors which, of course, were soon deemed "too feminine" because women didn't "look like leaders." Women who were perceived as "putting too much effort into their appearance" were even seen as less qualified.[20] This is just one example of a double bind—a scenario where no matter what a woman does, she cannot win.

Don't Be Afraid to Talk About Diversity

At Reverb, we know diversity, equity, and inclusion are a must. Embracing diversity broadens our perspectives, creates better solutions for clients, and keeps us rooted in a shared philosophy of human dignity. We've actually lost business because we didn't have enough racial diversity among our consultants, and we're working hard to do better. This poses a challenge because finding consultants of different races and genders isn't always easy. That's not an excuse, but a reminder that the onus is on us (and every organization) to form meaningful relationships with people outside of our limited network so that we can get to know and attract people from diverse backgrounds.

As many founders do, I started hiring people I knew. The company initially grew from my close network, then through employee referrals. Referrals are wonderful, because they come from a trusted source. However, the risk of referrals is hiring people who "look like you." That's just what happened at Reverb, and I worried that we were becoming too homogeneous. I know that diverse teams perform better.

---

20 https://www.rewire.org/work/unspoken-rules-workplace-attire-women/, https://www.businessinsider.com/work-clothes-history-2018-6#the-1980s-took-workplace-fashion-trends-to-several-tubular-new-extremes-an-unsurprising-development-given-the-decades--penchant-for-big-perms-sequin-encrusted-garments-and-bright-colors-28

They are more creative, come up with better solutions, and of course can understand and reflect a broader group of customers.

When I realized that my efforts to attract more diverse team members weren't working as well or as quickly as I'd hoped, I asked some of my most-trusted advisors for help. I was surprised at how awkward it felt, even as a longtime HR professional, because I'm still not used to talking overtly about race. But I knew I had to get out of my comfort zone if I wanted things to be different.

Based on the advice I received, I told a few of my closest coaching colleagues that I was looking for more coaches of color. They responded with enthusiastic introductions to some of the most accomplished coaches I've ever met, all women of color. Most important, these women not only added racial and ethnic diversity but made our team better at what we do by introducing different backgrounds, points of view, and life experiences.

Recently, the head of HR for a large health-care organization contacted me specifically requesting a woman of color to coach one of her senior leaders, also a woman of color. I was thankful we didn't have to turn her away. I share these examples because many people are uncomfortable talking openly about what diversity means to them. I want to give you permission to be smarter each day when it comes to *DEI (Diversity, Equity, Inclusion)*. Talking authentically about diversity requires us to ask hard questions and have uncomfortable conversations. Don't let embarrassment or the risk of making a mistake prevent you from asking for help.

Let's Look at Male Privilege

Talking about male privilege is not about bashing or discrediting men. It's about encouraging men to be part of the solution. I have had many male sponsors over the years who noticed my commitment and hard work and took it upon themselves to guide me, share candid feedback, and advocate on my behalf. They recommended me for stretch assignments and promotions. They recognized me, both publicly and privately. They made me better and helped me advance my career more rapidly than I could have without their support. They recognized the advantages they had and used their influence to help me and other women get opportunities we might not have otherwise. These men were true advocates and allies, though I didn't have the language to describe them that way at the time.

It's also true that *unrecognized* male privilege continues to hinder the progress, confidence, and wellness of many capable, talented, and hardworking women. This cannot be overstated. Amy Nelson, founder of The Riveter, a female-forward co-working space, describes how men in leadership can become better advocates: "The men who lead so many of Seattle's largest companies and most esteemed venture capital firms must stand in the gap (you name it—gender pay gap, advancement gap) and advocate for female leadership to make their business ideas a reality."[21]

Many of the women featured here, including me, have grown up in male-dominated industries. Technology companies and startups have been shaped by men for decades. Office fun meant playing ping-pong, decorating with Star Trek posters, and having beers—things that generally appeal to fewer women than men.[22] Modern-day technology companies are increasingly aware that a stereotypically masculine atmosphere can have a negative impact on building diverse teams. When people see an environment that doesn't speak to them,

---

21 Amy Nelson, "A Look Back to Look Forward: Why Highlighting Diverse Stories Matters," *GeekWire*, October 27, 2018, https://www.geekwire.com/2018/look-back-look-forward-highlighting-diverse-stories-matters/.

22 https://www.washington.edu/news/2015/02/11/how-to-interest-girls-in-computer-science-and-engineering-shift-the-stereotypes/

they get a sense of not fitting in and thereby feeling uncomfortable, which makes it less likely they'll join that company or stay long term if they do. Savvy companies are learning to make their spaces more welcoming and productive for all kinds of people, while simultaneously educating their workforce about how to break unconscious bias and increase belonging.

Imagine you're a sought-after female engineer who's being recruited by several companies. How would it feel to go through an entire day of interviews without meeting even *one* woman from the company? Would it make you wonder if the culture embraces women, if you're even going to fit in with the team? Kristin Toth Smith, COO of Seattle startup Dolly, described the challenges of being the only woman on her executive team. When the company was creating its maternity leave policy, all eyes were on her. She didn't see it as her responsibility to drive the policy just because she was a woman. She saw it as a leadership decision that everyone should have an equal part in crafting.[23]

Why "Fail Fast" Is Not Inclusive

In order to encourage experimentation and risk-taking, innovative companies and startups of all kinds embrace failure as part of their ethos. Failure is hard, and yet culturally we love the story of the person who initially failed but ultimately succeeded. We like the outcome, but not the process: while failure is in motion, it can be isolating and lonely.

Dave Parker, whom I call a startup guru, explains how even the much-loved value "fail fast" is not an inclusive concept. "Failure and all of the connotations that go with it are often culturally relevant. Two

---

23   Kristin Toth Smith, "The Value of a Gender Diversified Leadership Team with Kristin Toth Smith," interview presented at the Seattle HR Collective Meetup, Seattle, WA, January 10, 2018.

views are at the extremes: 'You didn't fail; it was a learning experience' and 'Failure is not an option.'

"A learning experience is great when you have a safety net: if someone in your family has capital that you can fall back on, or you know there is a job in a family or friend network and you know someone will hire you. When you don't have a safety net, you lean toward 'failure is not an option,' which likely means that you have to figure out how to make a bad situation work in spite of the circumstances. You can't leave your day job, so you have to work a side hustle.

"People with privilege ask why you're not committed to considering the option of failing fast, because they don't understand you may be the solo wage earner for your family. Killing bad ideas fast is a way to learn without betting the farm. Some people will read this and think I'm just parsing words or taking a nuance . . . they usually come from privilege."[24]

What Is Wage Equity, and What Does It Have to Do with Privilege?

Gender pay equity is a critical topic that companies are only now beginning to address. It refers to women being paid less than men for performing the same job. One reason women don't always fight for equal pay is because they often see themselves as less qualified. Another is that they may not know for certain whether they are being paid less than their male peers. Women need to keep asking for what they're worth, *and* leaders need to make sure women are paid the same, whether they ask for it or not. Once again, things are changing, but there's still a tremendous gap.

According to Lydia Frank, VP Content Strategy at PayScale,

---

24   Dave Parker, "Can I Get Your Expert Comment?," email to author, September 26, 2018.

"The reason white men have typically done well within the existing system is because it was built by them and for them. The way you advance in the workplace so often comes down to who you know in power, who has influence over your career trajectory, rather than your track record of results. When trying to mitigate bias in your pay and promotion practices, employers would do well to lean into utilizing data, technology, and standardized processes. If employers rely less on those relationship factors, such as who you know or who has influence over your career, and more on hard data, they will do a better job of standardizing the yardstick by which workers are measured in terms of their value to the organization."[25] Fortunately today we have tools like PayScale and Syndio that can help eradicate pay inequity.

Government can play a role, too. In March 2018, Washington State passed the Equal Pay Opportunity Act with the goal of ensuring equal pay for all genders during hiring and promotions. Along with other states, Washington has made it illegal to base a difference in pay on an employee's salary history[26] as one way to end the cycle of pay discrimination, which has historically kept women's wages below those of men regardless of qualifications and experience. Emily Parkhurst was recently named the market president and publisher for the *Puget Sound Business Journal*. She says, "I know for a fact that in previous jobs, I've been paid less than my male colleagues. This happened many times in my career."

When Erin Jones was promoted to assistant state superintendent of the State of Washington, she was given the biggest pay raise of her

---

25 Lydia Frank, "Would You Provide an Expert Comment?," email to author, November 20, 2018.

26 "Equal Pay Opportunity Act," Washington State Department of Labor & Industries, accessed December 10, 2018, https://www.lni.wa.gov/WorkplaceRights/Wages/PayReq/EqualPay/default.asp.

life, but in her second month, she learned she was making $10,000 *less* than the next lowest-paid cabinet member. When she confronted the powers that be, they said that her age and lack of experience was reflected in her salary. Yet the duties she performed were the same as, if not more than, her colleagues.

In a *Money* magazine article, "Women Have Pushed for Equal Pay for Decades. It's Sad How Little Progress We've Made," the authors share statistics that define the *gender pay gap*—women in America "make $0.80 on the dollar compared to their male counterparts. That gap is wider for black and Hispanic women, who earn 62.5% and 54.4%, respectively, of the paychecks their male colleagues receive."[27] Today women are not only standing up for themselves but backing each other publicly in an unprecedented fashion. When it was exposed that women were paid significantly less than men at the BBC, women joined forces as a sisterhood to support one another in asking for pay raises. Pay can be corrected, but it will be years before the BBC can earn back the trust that was lost when its secretive and illegal pay culture was exposed.[28]

Gender Pay Gap and Race

I recently listened to the podcast *Battle Tactics for Your Sexist Workplace* and learned that it's racist (yes, they used that word) to use *one* number to quantify the gender wage gap, since the gap varies dramatically by

---

27 Jennifer Calfas, "Women Have Pushed for Equal Pay for Decades. It's Sad How Little Progress We've Made," Money, April 10, 2018, http://time.com/money/5225986/equal-pay-day-2018-gender-wage-gap/.

28 Joanna Williams, "The BBC Sisterhood Has Made the Ultimate Sacrifice—and Asked for a Pay Rise | Coffee House," *The Spectator*, July 24, 2017. https://blogs.spectator.co.uk/2017/07/the-bbc-sisterhood-has-made-the-ultimate-sacrifice-and-asked-for-a-pay-rise/.

race.[29] White women are still getting paid more on average. To address this issue for all women, my colleagues and I on the Seattle HR Collective organized a panel about pay equity. The first three panelists we considered were all white. The irony did not escape me. We had to dig deeper and expand the list to better represent those who are most affected by this issue. When business development executive and DEI advocate Carolina Duclos joined our panel, she brought perspectives we couldn't have anticipated. Carolina told us people in her home country of Mexico talk openly about pay. They ask each other's salaries when they first meet. For people who are raised with that amount of pay transparency, imagine how surprised they are when having to negotiate salaries in the United States.[30]

As any employee knows, there are a few pivotal events that affect pay—two of those are hiring and promotions. The other is merit increases. At Google, engineers are told to nominate themselves for promotions. It's not suprising that women weren't nominating themselves as often as men. Alan Eustace, head of engineering, addressed the problem by sending a company-wide email: "'We've noticed women aren't nominating themselves and, hey, you should be!'" Adding that simple step seemed to work, so Google repeated it for several months. Once when Eustace forgot to send the email, female nominations instantly decreased. Laszlo Bock, head of people operations at the time, described the email alert as "nudging, not nagging."[31] While an email alone can't change your culture, Google's proactive encouragement contributed to a measurable difference in women's behavior

---

29   Eula Scott Bynoe and Jeannie Yandel, "Want a Raise? First Call Your Cable Company," *Battle Tactics for Your Sexist Workplace*, https://radiopublic.com/battle-tactics-for-your-sexist-wo-WDReqE/ep/s1!d4bc1, n.d., accessed June 26, 2018.

30   Carolina Duclos, "Pay Equity—Gender and Beyond," panel discussion, October 17, 2017.

31   Manoush Zomorodi, "Google's Head of HR on Growth-Hacking Gender Equality at Work," Note to Self, April 28, 2015, https://www.wbez.org/shows/note-to-self/googles-head-of-hr-on-growthhacking-gender-equality-at-work/2ed78c85-a6af-42e6-934e-8059928fc9a7.

and in the number of women receiving promotions. This demonstrates how organizations that fail to take similar steps risk continuing to overlook qualified women.

Office Housework and Other Little Indignities

One of the Next Gen interviewees describes working for a property development firm where the two male owners would ask her to make coffee each day. "Actually, they didn't ask," she said. It was assumed that all "office housework" was her role. These tasks, like making coffee, ordering snacks, and doing dishes, fall to women too often. Additionally, there were five guys on her team who were assigned to high-profile projects, while she was stuck with "team-building" happy hours because she was "so good at planning events." Office housework creates an extra burden for women *and* takes up time they could use working on more critical, high-impact, high-visibility projects.

Emily talks about the "little indignities" women must deal with throughout the day that men don't encounter. "Women catalog these experiences, and they start to stack up," she says. Emily isn't shy about describing these injustices to men in positions of power. She wants them to know the added pressure women face. She says, "There's the question of how to dress each day, and how much makeup to wear because people comment on a woman's looks and clothes before her quality of work. There's also the *double standard*—women are called 'aggressive,' when we're really being assertive."

We're accused of talking too much, when we're actually saying very little." [32,33] While women talk more in informal groups, research shows that women speak for shorter periods and less frequently than men in professional settings. One reason is that it's typically harder for

---

32 http://time.com/4837536/do-women-really-talk-more/

33 https://www.theguardian.com/commentisfree/2018/feb/14/why-do-women-talk-so-much-google-autocomplete

women to get the floor, and when they do, they're often interrupted. In addition, women worry about being perceived as too dominant and will employ strategies including speaking softly and alternately speaking up, then self-censoring. Imagine all the ideas we miss out on, when women hold themselves back rather than participate in meetings.

Emily recalls, "Even today, construction is happening across the street and grids were put down. I'm wearing heels and can't walk across the grid, so I have to walk around the block. That's not the end of the world, but on top of it, someone makes an inappropriate comment about my body or catcalls. That happens probably 98% of the time. Men don't have this distraction. And they don't have to deal with this in business meetings either." She adds, "Privilege is being utterly unaware of what other people are experiencing and feeling, like it's not your concern." But, she says, "Don't get me wrong, I have privilege that I'm unaware of, too."

> **EMILY PARKHURST** SAYS:
> " . . . someone makes an inappropriate comment about my body or catcalls. That happens probably 98% of the time. Men don't have this distraction. And they don't have to deal with this in business meetings either."

How Does Male Privilege Impact Women?

As women strive for greater heights, it's important to understand how women are underestimated and how that very doubt affects their performance. One thing that's generally assumed in high-pressure corporate settings is that a woman will likely underperform. She'll break quickly from stress, or she won't be able to balance work and family.

When women's ability to do a good job is called into question, it can lead to women having less confidence. It's a vicious cycle. This is called *stereotype threat*, which is the assumption that a woman will underperform. Because of the scrutiny women are under, they internalize messages that they're not good enough and those beliefs subconsciously become part of their nature.

Clean-up or Crisis: Women Wanted

When women finally do break the *glass ceiling* and get hired for prominent positions, it's frequently because no man wants to face the immensity of the job that's being vacated. Women often get called into leadership roles when there's damage to clean up or a PR crisis in a company. Sometimes, an organization needs a leader to take the fall. Other times, they're trying to prove they are diverse and inclusive. Either way, women don't just get *fewer* leadership opportunities. Theirs are different—often riskier and with higher stakes. Prominent examples include CEOs such as Carly Fiorina of Hewlett-Packard and Marissa Mayer at Yahoo. Both struggled during high-profile corporate changes, where their resignations were eventually called for.

"'When you look at opportunities for leadership that one might describe as high-risk, women are more likely to be selected into that kind of role,'" says Marianne Cooper, a sociologist at the Clayman Institute for Gender Research at Stanford University.[34] Women are twice as likely as men to raise their hand to accept these kinds of roles. According to Cooper, we believe that women versus men often possess qualities that can make them more suitable in difficult situations.

---

34 Jena McGregor, "Congratulations, Theresa May. Now Mind That 'Glass Cliff,'" *The Washington Post*, July 12, 2016, https://www.washingtonpost.com/news/on-leadership/wp/2016/07/12/congratulations-theresa-may-now-mind-that-glass-cliff/?noredirect=on&utm_term=.cbcc7e9a0360.

Perhaps because they get fewer high-profile leadership opportunities, women are also willing to take a risk on these roles. " Researchers say that these types of positions leave women standing on a *glass cliff.* The glass cliff is a phenomenon studied by academics that shows a disproportionate number of women and minorities reaching positions of leadership at particularly precarious times."[35]

Aiko explained to me that women of color don't have the privilege of smashing a glass ceiling. She says, "Black women face a *concrete ceiling,* and it's not due to lack of ambition." *The Wall Street Journal* reports, "Black, Hispanic and Asian women are eager to reach high-level positions, even more so than their white female peers. . . . Of the women surveyed, 48% of women of color said they aspired to be a top executive, compared with 37% of white women." Annalisa Adams-Qualtiere, a longtime leader in HR departments, explains why advocates are needed. "'When I hear "glass ceiling," I think that's great, you can break through glass. When it is concrete, you need a door, and there need to be people on the other side of that door.'"[36]

White Privilege

White privilege is an everyday topic of discussion among marginalized groups, yet it's a new topic in many white households. White women have been fighting their own battles so hard that many of them haven't been attentive to the plight of black and brown women. Many white women assumed all women were united as sisters, but they are now

---

35 McGregor, "Congratulations, Theresa May."

36 Jo Piazza, "Women of Color Hit a 'Concrete Ceiling' in Business," *The Wall Street Journal,* September 27, 2016, Business section, https://www.wsj.com/articles/women-of-color-hit-a-concrete-ceiling-in-business-1474963440.

being asked to listen and learn how they've failed to support women of color. An article in *HuffPost* explains, "White privilege is a *systemic cultural reality* that I can either choose to ignore or choose to acknowledge and attempt to change. It has nothing to do with my worth as a person or my own personal struggle."[37]

Many women of color do not feel heard or represented by modern-day *feminism*. The 2017 Women's March, where an estimated two million women took to the streets following Trump's election, has been criticized as being the "White Women's March." Women of color and trans women have complained vocally about a lack of inclusion, and a general disregard for the issues that affect them. They felt the march focused too much on the needs of *cisgender* white women and failed to address *intersectional feminism*; in other words, the needs of all women. Writer S. T. Holloway, who attended the 2017 march, explained why she planned to skip the march in 2018. "In cities all over the U.S., black women, some I knew and some I didn't, expressed their frustrations over feeling as though their voices, their issues, and their concerns and causes weren't given nearly as much value as those of the majority."[38,39]

The 2017 Women's March was the largest single-day protest in US history.[40] Yet women of color asked, "Where have you been all this time? Why haven't you been fighting for and with us before now?" We will never be able to build safe, equitable, and productive workspaces and communities without bridging this racial divide.

When I was a child, Seattle public schools taught me that America was a melting pot—a place where everyone could assimilate and have

---

37 Howerton, "White Privilege Doesn't Mean What You Think It Means."

38 https://www.essence.com/culture/black-women-boycott-womens-march/

39 https://www.huffingtonpost.com/entry/why-this-black-girl-will-not-be-returning-to-the-womens-march_us_5a3c1216e4b0b0e5a7a0bd4b

40 https://www.mylifetime.com/she-did-that/the-womens-march-became-the-largest-single-day-protest-in-united-states-history-one-year-ago

an equal opportunity to pull themselves up by their bootstraps. Yet we were never taught how assimilation asks people to give up their own language, culture, and heritage, to more closely resemble the majority. When you're educated this way as a child, it can take a long time before you begin to challenge what you've learned, and even longer to unlearn those stories and replace them with the more painful and accurate history and realities of what it means to be a person of color or immigrant in the United States.

Academic Robin DiAngelo wrote a book called *White Fragility*, explaining how white people defend themselves when questioned about racism. In her book, DiAngelo poses many questions for white women to contemplate. One that stuck with me was when she asked readers to think about school desegregation. Which kids are bused, from which neighborhoods, and into which schools? Why aren't buses going the opposite direction? I've been thankful for so long that I grew up attending public schools in Seattle during a time of busing and desegregation. Even as a child, I knew that black and brown children were bused in to attend my neighborhood elementary school. But I never questioned why. For the next forty years of my life, until hearing DiAngelo's question, I had never been asked or thought to dig into what that meant and how it shaped my beliefs about so-called good and bad schools, good and bad neighborhoods. How it contributed to my own beliefs and unconscious biases about race.

Angela Hanks is a *Forbes* contributor and the economic success director at CLASP (Center for Law and Social Policy). She writes on Twitter, "Feeling a little weird about the #DemandMore hashtag. Black women don't face a wage gap because we've failed to demand more. Policy and racism and their intersections created the wage gap and we need policy change to close it #BlackWomensEqualPay."[41] Angela's comments show how unhelpful it can be to tell women (of any race) to just "keep speaking up" and "keep demanding more," regarding equal pay. Women *have* been doing that, with minimal success and increasing frustration, since the late 1800s.

When women of color address the racial aggressions they face, Ruchika says the response is often "How dare you!" White people can feel attacked, offended, and may resist accountability. This is especially true for white women, another example of *white fragility*. On NPR, DiAngelo named common responses she hears from white women when discussing racism: ". . . probably the classic one is I was taught to treat everyone the same. I don't see color. It's focusing on race that divides us. Oh, I'm not racist. I marched in the '60s. I was in the Peace Corps. I was in Teach for America. I took a trip to Costa Rica. I have multiracial grandchildren."[42]

To admit we did or said something hurtful can seem devastating—as though it will forever crush our self-image and wipe away the good we've done. Many white people have grown up striving for perfection. They want to be seen as good, moral people; however, when it comes to racial awareness, we all have to open our eyes to oppression and ask ourselves how we are contributing. We need to actively learn about our own biases and intentionally counter them through words and actions.

Another woman of color from the Next Gen talks about how much she values relationships. When she has to tell people they've offended

41   Angela Hanks, "Feeling a Little Weird about the #DemandMore Hashtag. Black Women Don't Face a Wage Gap Because We've Failed to Demand More. Policy and Racism and Their Intersections Created the Wage Gap and We Need Policy Change to Close It #BlackWomensEqualPay," Tweet, @AngelaHanks (blog), August 7, 2018, https://twitter.com/AngelaHanks/status/1026835822425894914.

42   "Robin DiAngelo On White People's 'Fragility,'" NPR.org, accessed December 9, 2018, https://www.npr.org/2018/08/18/639822895/robin-diangelo-on-white-peoples-fragility.

her, it's complicated. She explains that it's easier with gender than with race because she has lots of girlfriends around to validate when something isn't right. With race, it's harder because she's often the only person of color in a room. "When something happens that I don't like, I don't want to always bring it up because my voice will lose effect. I don't want people to think, '*Well, she thinks everything is problematic.*' The biggest thing for me has been choosing the moments because my goal is to bridge the gap and make change, and I won't be able to do that if I isolate myself from people because they are scared to be themselves around me. That's messed up in itself."

RUCHIKA TULSHYAN SAYS:
"I have to hide my authenticity on a daily basis—not sharing about myself, not feeling comfortable talking about my parents or the foods we like to eat. I fear being stereotyped or asked questions like 'Did you have an arranged marriage?' This is extremely burdensome." When I asked Ruchika how often she felt this way, she said she feels it *every single day*! I was honestly shocked.

Erin Jones mentions how in interviews, it's common for people to tell her, "You know, you are really articulate." Translation: You're really articulate for a black woman. At first, Erin didn't know how to respond. Soon, she formulated a potent reply.

ERIN JONES SAYS:
"Why, thank you. I can be articulate in French and Spanish as well, if you'd like."

On the *TED Radio Hour* from NPR, Jamila Lyiscott speaks about the common issue of calling women of color articulate, as if it's a novelty. She's a first-generation American who grew up in Brooklyn with parents from Trinidad. Jamila is currently working on her PhD in literature and race at Columbia. She says, "And so when someone calls me articulate, it's not so much that they've never heard someone put together some words very well. It's that coming from my body, coming from my skin, coming from me, it's suddenly impressive."[43]

These women's experiences are a direct call to action. Those in the majority need to do the hard work in order to educate themselves about what's offensive, invite people of color to be blunt with them, and build a thicker skin in order to receive feedback. This shifts the burden away from those who have been excluded and marginalized. If we allow people to remain isolated unless they are the ones to initiate the conversation, we're placing one more barrier in their way. Those in the majority must proactively seek out and listen to feedback and create safe spaces for these tough and important conversations.

Tools for Change

As a person of color who is constantly educating others and speaking out against bias and racial prejudice at work, Cheryl says, "I do a lot of training in order to have tools for difficult conversations and hard

---

43 Jamila Lyiscott, "What Does It Mean to Be 'Articulate'?," *TED Radio Hour*, November 14, 2014, https://www.npr.org/2014/11/14/362372282/what-does-it-mean-to-be-articulate.

moments. And I've actually built a curriculum around it for my company that we teach. To be honest, a lot of meditating goes into it. I sit down at the end of the day, and I write down and think through my responses, so I can understand what to say in the moment and what it means. It's a shame that I have to practice for moments like this, but I do. I also have mentors and a coach who I call to help me process." I wondered how Cheryl finds the words, courage, and wisdom to respond when she faces resistance.

CHERYL INGRAM SAYS:
"Most of the time, the goal is to educate. I meet the person where I think they are. I speak so they can understand the message. The second part is always to make sure I'm authentic, courageous, and I say what I need to say."

Cheryl has spent years practicing these hard conversations, so don't feel you need to hold yourself to the same standard overnight. Do, however, find a way to learn from her example, even if it means taking one step toward your own courageous and authentic style of confronting those with bias.

Cheryl told me a story from her perspective as a black woman that left me speechless. "I was giving a presentation to a leadership team in a large company. There were nine people in the room—three white women, five white men, and me. My presentation explained what it would take to have a DEI audit run in their company. It was an hour long, and they didn't have very many questions. At the end of the meeting, a man, the VP, stood up and said,

"Did he really just say that?"

'That was one of the best DEI presentations I've ever seen when it comes to an audit. You're a lot smarter than you look.'" Cheryl was appalled, momentarily stunned into silence, and thought to herself, *Did he really just say that?* She looked at him and scanned the room, where 70% of the heads were down.

First, Cheryl weighed her options—if she said nothing, she might get the account, and if she said something, she might not. She chose to speak up. Are you ready for it?

CHERYL INGRAM SAID:
"So here I am thinking that you could be racist, sizeist, or sexist. Whatever you think about me visibly, I'm wondering what triggered you. What made you think that it was okay to say that? It's never ever okay to say something like that to anyone, and I hope that in the future you don't."

The room fell silent, and then after a long pause one woman in the crowd spoke up. "Yeah, we should stop saying that to people in our company." The VP turned red, apologized, and walked out of the room. That same woman approached Cheryl and said, "That's not the first time he's said that. It happens frequently, and you're the first person who has ever spoken up to him. You empowered me to do the same, and I really appreciated that." Cheryl didn't get that account, but that was OK with her. After the way he behaved, who would want it? She did, however, serve as a role model and inspiration to every individual in that room who had silently tolerated the VP's caustic verbal attacks without speaking up.

Owning Privilege and Holding on to Respect

When she does equity work, Erin Jones says she always starts by owning her privilege. She was raised by white parents in Europe, speaks four languages, went to private schools, and is a jock and academic who runs her own public speaking business. You might guess these privileges shield her from racism, yet if she's in her basketball clothes in a neighborhood where she doesn't live, she is treated the same as any other black person without all those privileges. It was sad and surprising for me to hear that Erin has never participated in casual Fridays. I thought those were days when everyone at work could feel comfortable and be themselves. She explains, "I didn't want to give up any level of respect." Erin told me an unforgettable story that I'd like to share with you:

"I had just been promoted to serve as assistant state superintendent. Superintendent Randy Dorn was scheduled to keynote at the superintendents' conference, which was being held in Yakima at the convention center. A couple of weeks before the event, he had a conflict arise and asked if I would be willing to speak in his place."

Yakima is a small town with an urban population just under 100,000, only an hour's drive south of scenic Mt. Rainier. Located in central Washington State, Yakima is known as farm country. Fueled by agriculture, the region produces some of the finest apples, pears, cherries, corn, and peppers in the country. Its wine country has even become a bit of a tourist attraction. The region is nearly 50% white, 45% Hispanic, and less than 2% black. It's not hard to imagine Erin standing out in the crowd.

"I was so honored. This would be my first big keynote. My mom and dad had just moved to the United States after careers as teachers in the Netherlands. Mom offered to drive with me, both to keep me company and because she had never been to Eastern Washington. I put on my best suit and heels and jewelry. We had a great trip over. It was our first long trip together since I had moved to the United States almost twenty years earlier. When we arrived at the convention center, I had butterflies in my stomach, but I was actually very excited to speak. Mom and I walked into the lobby. A tall woman in a suit came walking toward us. She looked right at my mother and said, 'You must be our keynote. Welcome!' I was so confused. Mom looked like her head was going to explode.

"Mom pointed up at my face (she's 5'2" on a good day) and said in her momma-bear voice, 'This is my daughter, Erin Jones, and *SHE* is your keynote today . . . Erin, give me your keys,' and she stormed out of the building. The woman apologized quietly but seemed absolutely unaware of the thing she had just done. She brought me into the auditorium, where, from the back, all I could see was bald heads and gray hair. What Superintendent Dorn had failed to tell me was that this was a conference for superintendents for rural/remote school districts. There may have been two other women in that room. The average age was sixty. This was not a demographic I knew well after a career in urban, Title I schools. What did I have to share that would resonate for them? I began to doubt myself.

"When it came time for me to begin, I just spoke from my heart. I shared my WHY for becoming a teacher. When I was finished, I received a standing ovation. I guess my story resonated. I looked out in the audience to see my mother. She was nowhere to be found. When I was done, I looked out in the lobby for her. She was not there, either. I remembered I had given her my car keys, so I went to the car. She was sitting in the passenger seat. It was obvious she had been crying. As I got into the car, here are the words my mother said to me that I will never forget: 'I realized today that maybe if you were not my daughter, I might not see you, either.' Deep! We both cried for a long time before driving back across the mountains. That day would change us forever."

People You Are Not Likely to See

Privilege means there are people you are not likely to see—either you don't physically see them, or you can't imagine them in leadership roles. Erin's mother realized that she's always seen Erin as having incredible potential because Erin is her daughter. She knows what Erin is capable of achieving. Are there whole groups of people whose potential you have written off because you had no exposure to them as individuals and no idea what they're capable of? Are there stereotypes and implicit biases you've internalized without realizing it, that have caused you to miss the possibility, creativity, and ingenuity of those around you? These are crucial questions to ask yourself in order to challenge your own unconscious biases.

Imposter Syndrome: Never Good Enough

Professional women often suffer from the *opposite* of entitlement: *imposter syndrome*. It's the internal sense that you're not good enough, or you don't deserve something, regardless of the evidence that you are more than qualified. It's when you think you need another degree or a bigger title to deserve what you've already accomplished or to earn acceptance and recognition from your colleagues. For many women of all races, no amount of awards or accomplishments are enough to make them feel like the experts they really are. That's because their feelings of self-doubt are constantly reinforced by society. Even former First Lady Michelle Obama acknowledged feeling that she wasn't good enough. One of the psychologists who coined the term *imposter syndrome* has said that approximately 70% of people will experience impostor syndrome to varying degrees at some point in their lives.[44]

---

44   Lila MacLellan, "Michelle Obama Has Imposter Syndrome, Too—and Some Advice for Dealing with It," *Quartz at Work*, December 7, 2018, https://qz.com/work/1486790/michelle-obamas-smart-advice-for-dealing-with-imposter-syndrome/.

Author and researcher Brené Brown shares how imposter syndrome and perfectionism are linked. "'If I look perfect, live perfect, work perfect, I can avoid or minimize criticism, blame, and ridicule.'"[45] That's a lie we commonly tell ourselves, that gets in the way of accepting that we're only human, we're fallible, and that's OK.

KIERAN SNYDER NOTES:
"When leaders lose sight of their privilege, they lose empathy and feel entitled to success."

Imposter syndrome creates an invisible fence that prohibits advancement. Imposter syndrome makes it difficult for women to support one another, transcend differences, and truly connect. Let that sink in for a moment—by doubting our greatness, we give up the ability to connect with those around us. Aiko reminded me

"Women easily convince themselves that we have nothing to bring to the table in these relationships. That is so far from true."

that imposter syndrome supports the scarcity model (the belief that there's not enough to go around), and yet, I still fall into this trap myself. Last summer, a journalist from *The Wall Street Journal* wanted to interview me. When I looked at who she had previously featured, I saw people with big titles and important roles, and I wondered, "Why would she want to hear my story?" I saw myself as less accomplished, and yet I've worked for some of the biggest brands in the world. My

---

45   Lynn Okura, "Brené Brown: Perfectionism Is the 20-Ton Shield We Use to Protect Ourselves," video, Huffington Post, October 5, 2013, OWN section, https://www.huffingtonpost.com/2013/10/05/brene-brown-perfectionism-shame-oprah_n_4045358.html.

experience carries weight, and I had to consciously remind myself of that. Do you see how imposter syndrome holds us back? I would not claim to have conquered it, but I have learned to recognize when I'm feeling like an impostor and talk myself down.

Imposter syndrome snuck up on me again at an elite event in Seattle—a who's who of the tech industry. The attendees were mostly middle-aged, wealthy, white, male entrepreneurs and investors. Many of these folks can be hard to connect with, because everyone wants to know them; they are sought after for advice and influence. There are others in that group who are among my biggest champions. Regardless, I found myself feeling intimidated and insignificant. I thought, "These guys seem to have it all. Their influence and power make them unapproachable. Everyone wants their time. It feels like a boys' club." That kind of thinking has a negative effect on women's confidence. Women easily convince themselves that we have nothing to bring to the table in these relationships. That is so far from true.

Often people who are underrepresented take a big risk when confronting injustice, and it helps them when others join in, so let's talk solutions. Are you ready to create positive change? We all have opportunities to take concrete steps, big and small. Let's explore how you can take personal responsibility for creating spaces that are safe, welcoming, and inclusive for everyone. The following actions will help you become a better advocate.

6 WAYS TO USE YOUR PRIVILEGE FOR GOOD

#1 Identify Your Unconscious Biases; We All Have Them

Despite your role or position, seek out diversity training for yourself and approach it with gusto. It's easy to find online programs, podcasts, books, and educational events. Cheryl Ingram's firm Diverse City has a video training series you can watch on diversity and unconscious bias.[46] Don't wait for your company to offer training. Find it and feel good about educating yourself.

If you are in a position to help introduce unconscious bias and diversity training at your organization, do it. Suggest ways to make the culture more inclusive. Take steps to set goals that will increase diversity and inclusion company wide.

#2 Act on Your Best Intentions

If you don't know where to start, do some research. Ask a couple of people who don't have the same privilege as you what they need or what gets in their way. Dedicate yourself to learning and creating change. No step is too small. Aiko reminds us, "Showing empathy should not become charity or a disempowering gesture to the person whom you intend to support. You should be disrupting bias power systems because they are discriminatory and biased, not because that 'poor person' needs your help."

Kieran tells a story about her male colleague at Microsoft who subtly made sure she was given the spotlight. "We were in a meeting with senior executives. It was the typical setting where we were on one side of the table facing the executives on the other side. I did 85% of the talking because it was my

---

46   "Diverse City LLC YouTube Channel," YouTube, accessed December 13, 2018, https://www.youtube.com/channel/UCq51AR3RAEmstQbY6h1ONmA. Find more resources and blog entries on Diverse City's website: "Diverse City LLC," Diverse City LLC, accessed December 13, 2018, https://diversecityllc.com/.

presentation to run, but 100% of the responses were directed at my colleague. Because I have a strong personality, I wasn't used to this. It was really frustrating. My colleague did something remarkable. He walked to the other side of the table with his laptop and sat next to the executives, as if to show them an answer to their question on his screen. Then, he never moved back. This put the visual focus entirely on me." Kieran notes, "We really needed that meeting to go well. I didn't have to call anyone out, and neither did he. He is a good example of being an *ally* to women." With one simple gesture, he found a way to become an advocate and shift the focus where it belonged, to Kieran.

#3 Give Yourself Permission to Make Mistakes; Then Accept Accountability

We have all likely said or done something that had an unintended impact. It's natural to feel defensive, and at the time, you might not understand why your words landed the way they did. You may struggle even after some amount of reflection. Keep an open mind and realize that feelings of guilt, anger, or shame are not productive. Aiko suggests, "These feelings may not be productive, but they *are normal*. Allow yourself to feel them, then move toward self-empowerment." Men might feel as if they are walking on eggshells when they are trying to grasp women's challenges, just as I might feel when trying to understand the experiences of people of color. Accept this reality as you go through these growing pains.

Next time you feel defensive, let it be a signal to get curious and focus on what is actionable. Ask questions. Make some mistakes. Rather than staying silent, ask yourself, "What can

I learn, how can I help, and what will I do differently going forward?" Don't let defensiveness shut you down. Be vulnerable and take the risk of engaging in hard conversations. Discomfort is inevitable, but we'll all be better for it.

#4 Life Hack: Reject Stereotypes

I get a kick out of seeing my daughter become a fierce rock climber. She likes taking selfies while flexing her arm muscles. Her ideal body image is one that's strong. This is healthier and more empowering than wanting to be pretty, cute, or skinny. I've always despised calling girls "princess." It perpetuates a stereotype that doesn't embody power, intelligence, or agency. Author Sarah Lacy agrees. She says, "Don't call your daughter a princess. Substitute something else. Lately, I've been using 'president.'"[47]

In a study about what people search online when no one is looking, gender stereotypes are prevalent. Google search results suggest that "contemporary American parents are far more likely to want their boys smart and their girls skinny."[48]

- For every 10 U.S. Google queries about boys being overweight, there are 17 queries about girls. (In reality, boys are 9% more likely to be overweight than girls.)

- For every 10 U.S. Google queries about girls being gifted, there are about 25 queries for boys. (In reality, girls are about 11% more likely to be in a gifted program.)

47   Sarah Lacy, "FFA Presents: Summer Sips with Sarah Lacy, Founder/CEO of Pando Daily and Chairman Mom," July 11, 2018.

48   Seth Stephens-Davidowitz, "Opinion | Google, Tell Me. Is My Son a Genius?," *The New York Times*, December 20, 2017, Opinion section, https://www.nytimes.com/2014/01/19/opinion/sunday/google-tell-me-is-my-son-a-genius.html.

These attitudes and stereotypes not only pervade parenting, they impact the expectations of the teachers and coaches who work with our kids every day. They're embedded in our songs, movies, commercials, and other media, which makes them inescapable. Girls take these messages to heart and grow up wanting to be liked and accepted over being smart and accomplished. This puts them out of sync with their intellect and interests.

An inspiring video by Oiselle, a female-founded women's running apparel company, shows how women's historic obedience has evolved into empowerment and independence. "When we were girls, they taught us to obey. They taught us to look pretty and not cause trouble. They told us to be nice. When we

> *"Girls take these messages to heart and grow up wanting to be liked and accepted over being smart and accomplished."*

met the heroes, they didn't look like us, they didn't move like us, they didn't follow rules like us." Juxtapose that with today: "We tell the stories, we create the tradition, and it doesn't look like the old school. We will not be compared or pitted against or trained to seek approval. We will take up space and we will know greatness when we feel it."[49]

Many of us are still learning to allow gender and sexuality to exist on a spectrum. We're seeing people as individuals, instead of fixed identities, but there's still work to do. Salesforce offers a positive example of how to honor LGBTQIA+

---

49   Oiselle, *Oiselle New School*, accessed October 22, 2018, https://www.youtube.com/watch?v=LfSjiMJzOlI&feature=youtu.be.

employees. When Indiana passed a religious freedom law that would limit gay rights, Salesforce, the largest tech company in the state, quickly announced that they would cancel all programs requiring employees or customers to travel to Indiana. CEO Marc Benioff said this public stance enhanced Salesforce's internal culture as well.[50]

#5 Open Doors to Create Opportunity

Here are a few ways to open doors for women at work.

- Research how you can be an advocate; then ask for their input.

- Listen to and believe their stories.

- Give them the floor and reinforce their points.

- Take their opinions seriously and amplify them.

- Offer them deals, just as you would for white men.

- Pay them equally, even if they ask for less or made less in the past.

- Give key people an opportunity to meet this under-accessed talent pool.

- Offer public praise, early and often.

- Challenge those who put them down or don't take them seriously.

50   Richard Waters, "Salesforce Chief Who Took on Bible Belt Is Ranked Top LGBT Ally," *Financial Times*, October 24, 2016, https://www.ft.com/content/39ed5a3a-91f7-11e6-a72e-b428cb934b78.

Early in her career, Leslie had a female manager who hired a speech coach for her because she was struggling with English as a second language. He taught her to recognize there's very little space in between sentences when speaking with a group of men. "No one pauses for you to say something. You have to interject." This one-on-one coaching was helpful to Leslie. Today, men are being asked to make space for women's voices and to realize when they are dominating the conversation.

At a lunch for startup HR leaders, an HR manager raised her hand. "We have a twenty-five-person sales team made up of all men, and we're hiring the first woman. What should we do to make her feel included?" We all laughed and said, "How about hire two?" It was kind of a joke, but kind of not. When a group lacks diversity, it can be difficult to introduce the first person who's different from the rest. It's not just about how the newcomer will adjust, it's also about the group changing its norms and learning to be inclusive and welcoming to someone who's different from them.

#6 Address Inappropriate Comments— Silence Is Not an Option

When she sees a person say or do something that causes even minor harm or discomfort, Christy says she tries to assume positive intent. "I really have to check my temper when things like this happen, but I often start with 'Hey, can I see you for a second?'" She'll pull the person aside and let them try to save face. She says people frequently know when they've done something offensive. They'll try to explain it away as being an inside joke or innocent gesture of fun.

When they're finished making excuses, she says, "Look, when you did *this*, it made me feel like *this*." She closes the dialogue with "Please don't do that again." Regardless of intent, it's important for people to understand the impact of their words and actions.

It can be hard to respond when you're on the receiving end of hurtful or derogatory comments. We go to work expecting people to behave like mature adults, but sometimes they surprise us by being abusive or disrespectful. When I've been targeted with yelling or outrageous remarks, I found myself shocked into silence. I heard them, but my mind convinced me that "They're not really saying this right now." Realizing that my reaction in the moment was not helping me change the situation eventually prompted me to create a strategy. I couldn't predict when something outrageous would happen, but I could be ready. I asked myself, "What do I want to say when someone is rude, hostile, or aggressive? How do I want to show up?" I decided on two goals: Stay calm / don't get flustered; and ask to speak to them in private, when we're both prepared to have a more constructive conversation. Now when I'm shocked, I'm no longer silent; I'm ready to respond.

Guys—you too must confront men when they dismiss female colleagues, interrupt, or make insensitive remarks. Set the tone for respectful behavior. Communicate clearly what kind of behavior will and will not be tolerated. You don't have to have all the answers—just guts and integrity. Your advocacy is crucial. If you're already an advocate, teach the next guy who's not as "woke" as you.

As a Jewish woman, Teri has overheard hostile,

anti-Semitic remarks. The way she's chosen to handle them works well in confronting any kind of bias or discrimination. She remembers a colleague saying, "If there were any Jews in this room, I would know." This reminded me of the scene in the movie *BlacKkKlansman*, where the founder of the KKK, David Duke, says he would know a black person by the sound of their voice.[51] He's not aware that the man on the other end of the line is a black police officer. When Teri heard that remark, she didn't have the skills to respond appropriately, but today, she'd say, "How would you know? What do you mean? Tell me about that very interesting comment you just made."

What We Have to Learn

I recently took my daughter to an exhibit that included my friend Michael Maine's performance art piece on the dismantling of black culture. His mom Diane Maine was there, and as a black woman raised in the South, she talked about how she was not allowed to speak as class valedictorian. When Diane thanked Sidonie for caring, my daughter replied, "You shouldn't have to thank me for caring. That's my responsibility. It's so sad you even have to thank me." At thirteen years old, my daughter is aware of privilege that many of us in our forties and fifties are only just now realizing. That gives me hope for the future.

---

51 Spike Lee, *BlacKkKlansman*.

IMPLICIT ASSOCIATION TEST (IAT)

I'd like to recommend a tool to help you uncover some of your unconscious biases. It is called the Implicit Association Test (IAT). This free online tool lets you assess your bias in categories such as gender, race, religion, disability, age, weight, and how you associate weapons with race. Recognizing that you have bias and blind spots is essential to personal growth. Discovering these uncomfortable truths about ourselves is a goal of an organization called Project Implicit.[52] They aim to learn more about the thoughts and feelings that are outside of our conscious awareness and control. Their findings serve to educate people about hidden biases, provide a virtual laboratory for collecting data about bias, and develop strategies to combat unwanted bias. Please consider taking the IAT. Discuss your results with someone who can help you be accountable to the changes you need to make—a friend, colleague, *mentor,* or coach.

We have so much to learn from each other. Sexism, racism, and all forms of discrimination are ingrained forces keeping us apart. For many people, work is where we encounter the most diversity because our neighborhoods, places of worship, and friend groups are often made up of people who look like us. Change begins when we discover what it's like to walk in each other's shoes and adapt our behavior accordingly. Remember, it takes courage, vulnerability, and humility

---

52 Project Implicit is a nonprofit organization and international collaboration between researchers who are interested in implicit social cognition—thoughts and feelings outside of conscious awareness and control. The goal of the organization is to educate the public about hidden biases and to provide a "virtual laboratory" for collecting data on the Internet.

to admit what you don't know and experiment with new behaviors. Change might happen more slowly than we wish, but we can all start with ourselves.

Next we're going to explore sexual harassment and abuse of power in the workplace. The #MeToo movement has freed the voices of people who have been targets of harassment and abuse. Sexual assault must be addressed with speed and consequences. It cannot be tolerated in the workplace, or anywhere. These aren't easy topics, yet we have to talk about them in order to do better. Let's keep going.

END-OF-CHAPTER CHECKLIST: **PRIVILEGE**

> *"Ask for what you want, need, and*
> *deserve—if not for yourself, then for*
> *the sake of women who will follow."*

Mid-Career and Next Gen Women:

☐ Prepare and practice. Write down what you'll say when you experience or witness inappropriate behavior at work, so you're ready to respond. Practice the words, and role-play with someone you trust. That way, you don't have to worry about being quick on your feet when the time comes.

☐ When things are tough, share your story with trusted friends. Why? To remind yourself that you don't have to go through this alone. If you're vulnerable with the right people, they will support you.

☐ Ask for what you want, need, and deserve—if not for yourself, then for the sake of women who will follow. Many women find it difficult to negotiate salary, ask for a raise, or request a promotion. But it's often easier to ask on behalf of others.

☐ Use *amplification* to give voice to women's ideas, including your own. Develop a buddy system with one or more female colleagues to reinforce each other's comments and suggestions in meetings. Don't allow *hepeating* and *mansplaining* to go unchallenged.

☐ Do not write off or invalidate experiences that others see as unjust. Be mindful of any tendency to correct, silence, talk over, undermine, exclude, or give unwanted advice. People are the experts of their own experience.

☐   Engage in difficult conversations about privilege. Give yourself permission to be imperfect. It's better to learn from your mistakes and take responsibility than to remain silent.

Male Advocates:

☐   When you read the experiences of women in this book, notice how the women in your life have been similarly impacted. Offer them compassion. Honor the energy and fortitude that's required to be a woman. Notice how male privilege has eased your success. Allow yourself to feel humbled. Listen to women. Believe them. Fight for them.

☐   Create space for women's voices. Ask women questions, give them the floor, and reinforce their perspective, all the while giving them credit. If someone interrupts a woman in a meeting, tell them you'd like to hear her complete her thought before moving on.

☐   Ask one or two female colleagues how you can support them. You may be surprised at the ways you can use your power to help them succeed.

HR, DEI, and Other Business Leaders:

☐   Develop a comprehensive DEI plan that includes policies, training, advocacy, and safe spaces. Don't attempt to check the box by doing only one of these—you will fail.

☐ Discuss diversity, equity, and inclusion on a company-wide basis and at team meetings. Help employees understand that diversity is an important part of your values and policies, as well as a key driver of business results. One small but visible step toward inclusion is using people's preferred *pronouns* (she/her/hers or they/them/theirs) in meetings and on team websites.

☐ Start and support Employee Resource Groups (ERGs)—by race, gender, sexual orientation, for parents and others. Keep intersectionality in mind. Provide sponsorship, funding, and time for employees to participate. Don't make them do all the work on their own.

☐ Teach leaders inclusive facilitation skills. Otherwise, who speaks up, who remains quiet, and who dominates conversations is left to chance.

☐ Train recruiters and hiring managers about unconscious bias, since they are the gatekeepers for those who will join your organization. Adopt tools that help remove bias from interviewing and hiring.

15

#METOO

I n the fall of 2017, sexual harassment and sexual assault victims came out in droves to share their "MeToo" stories and name the perpetrators involved. So far, more than 250 powerful celebrities, politicians, and CEOs have had allegations made against them—Harvey Weinstein, Bill Cosby, Louis C.K., Kevin Spacey, Charlie Rose, and Matt Lauer, to name a few. With people of all genders voicing their horrific experiences, people all over the world including the United States, Europe, and Asia are demanding awareness and action against predatory behavior. Xiong Jing, director of the Beijing-based Women's Media Monitor Network, said, "'You could say it's a shift—or that it's erupting like a volcano.'"[53]

The #MeToo movement is changing the way we conduct ourselves at work. It's given everyone a heightened sense of caution with their words and actions. It's opened our eyes to what's really going on around us. Inappropriate comments, sexual innuendos, and unwanted sexual advances can no longer be tolerated, though sadly many women have grown accustomed to them. Companies are adopting and reinforcing zero tolerance, anti-harassment, and anti-discrimination policies. They're teaching leaders to effectively address these situations, often for the first time.

---

53 James Griffiths, "Women in China Face Unique #MeToo Challenges, but See Some Progress," CNN, July 27, 2018, https://www.cnn.com/2018/07/27/asia/me-too-china-intl/index.html.

Tarana Burke founded the #MeToo movement in 2006 to help survivors of sexual violence "find pathways to healing."[54] She explains that sexual violence is not just about sex. "It's about power. And it's about the abuse of power."[55]

> *"In light of #MeToo, some men have decided to just avoid working with women as much as possible."*

Let's debunk some #MeToo myths and answer a few common questions (Hint: the answers are all YES):

- Can men and women still meet alone in an office with the door closed?

- Is it OK to travel on business with members of the opposite sex?

- Are colleagues still free to date, as long as they're not in a direct reporting relationship or violating company policy?

In light of #MeToo, some men have decided to just avoid working with women as much as possible. This fear that drives them to exclude women is not to be taken lightly. If men stop meeting, mentoring, and including women, it will stifle progress for generations of high-potential women. No man in the wake of #MeToo was fired for having a meeting with a woman, giving a tasteful compliment, or offering an

---

54   "About | Me Too," Me Too Movement, accessed October 27, 2018, https://metoomvmt.org/about/.

55   Ashley Velez, "#MeToo Founder Tarana Burke Breaks Down Why Bill Clinton's Affair with Monica Lewinsky Was an Abuse of Power," *The Root*, October 16, 2018, https://www.theroot.com/metoo-founder-tarana-burke-breaks-down-why-bill-clinto-1829795624.

appropriate, platonic hug. As diversity and engagement leader Amelia Ransom said on a panel discussion I moderated, "No one in the #MeToo movement ever said, 'He hugged me.'"[56] Some women, however, have complained about hugs that feel inappropriate or forced.

I get a lot of questions from male leaders asking what is now unacceptable, since #MeToo has entered our lexicon: "Can I still compliment a woman's hair or sweater? Can I still ask a woman out or open the door for her?" Ruchika points at opposite ends of the spectrum to remind us that no one has been investigated, incarcerated, or fired for flirting. While I agree we need to clarify what appropriate behavior looks like, the line is and has always been quite clear. If you're unsure, use these simple guidelines: "Would I say this in front of my spouse, daughter, mother, or a customer? Would I want this to show up in the press or on Twitter?" If you want to compliment women on their clothing and hairstyles, do you share similar compliments with men?

> *"Would I say this in front of my spouse, daughter, mother, or a customer? Would I want this to show up in the press or on Twitter?"*

In the first chapter, we talked about power in terms of privilege. That helps us approach the #MeToo conversation with context. We know those who have power are frequently held to different standards. They don't suffer consequences as everyone else does. They get to define what's morally correct, fair, and acceptable. When a person has power, they can utilize control tactics including threats, coercion, intimidation, denial, minimizing, and blame. They might even use verbal, emotional, physical, or economic abuse, all of which can be subtle or done in plain view. Recognizing and preventing these abuses of

---

56 Amelia Ransom, "Nike. Uber. Weinstein. What HR Needs in the Wake of #MeToo," panel discussion, August 8, 2018.

power are becoming integrated as essential topics in diversity, equity, inclusion, and workplace safety initiatives.

Every Woman Had a #MeToo Story

This summer, I was telling my daughter and her friend Clementine about my research for this book. I had just completed the interviews and was explaining the topics we covered. When I mentioned the #MeToo stories, Clementine's eyes grew wide. She asked innocently, "Did anyone have one?" When she heard that every single woman had one or more, her jaw dropped. She was rightfully shocked. Please take that in: all thirteen women had a #MeToo story. That's how prevalent workplace harassment is for professional women. Women of my generation have long accepted those behaviors as normal—not appropriate, but pervasive. It took many of the women I interviewed a decade or two before they were able to look back and recognize that they'd been enduring harassment without naming it. But younger women today have the information, vocabulary, and support to act with less hesitation. They are quicker to recognize impropriety and respond, whether calling it out or voting with their feet by leaving companies that don't support their right to a harassment-free workplace. For me, that was one of the most uplifting aspects of hearing from the Next Gen women.

#MeToo has become a catchall phrase used to describe what survivors of sexual harassment and abuse have endured. That doesn't mean the severity and consequences don't vary, but all of these experiences (leering, verbal abuse, coercion, sexual assault) fall in the #MeToo bucket for the purposes of this discussion. We'll begin with #MeToo stories and perspectives from the interviewees, then close with suggestions and solutions for change.

Cheryl Ingram says, "When the #MeToo movement started, the

conversation was rooted in how women were facing sexual harassment and how that was hurting their position. And not just sexual harassment, but the racial issues they were facing in their careers and in professional spaces from offenders and oppressors who were men, male-identified persons." A writer for *Open Democracy*, Lilian Calles Barger, expands on Cheryl's thought. "Although the most high-profile #MeToo stories have focused on celebrities or executives, most victims are disproportionately young, low-income, and minority women."[57]

Leanin.org reports that 60% of women say they've been sexually harassed.[58] These aren't incidents happening "somewhere else." They're happening right here in our workplaces. The people involved are no different from the women you see every day. #MeToo stories have emerged in just about every industry, from sports to the military, technology, politics, entertainment, and retail. It's long overdue that we expose this behavior and create environments where everyone feels safe and can be productive at work. All working professionals need a way to quickly report and resolve concerns when they've been bullied or abused.

It's Never Your Fault

Ruchika Tulshyan believes #MeToo still needs some differentiation between the extremes of assault versus flirting with a coworker. "Are they both #MeToo moments? Obviously not. #MeToo is about understanding that harassment, assault, and sexual abuse is really

---

57 Lilian Calles Barger, "What Came before #MeToo? The 'Himpathy' That Shaped Misogyny," openDemocracy, October 18, 2018, https://www.opendemocracy.net/transformation/lilian-calles-barger/what-came-before-metoo-himpathy-that-shaped-misogyny.

58 "Help Yourself—and Others—Cope with Sexual Harassment," Lean In, accessed October 27, 2018, https://leanin.org/sexual-harassment.

widespread. It's given us language, so we can speak openly and in a way that isn't hush-hush. For a long time, it was easy to dismiss harassing actions as something women just had to take. Women were encouraged to brush it off and to think, *It's kind of flattering, right?* And I think what's really great is now finally a lot of men even in my circles are like oh my gosh, yeah I can see where the problem with that is because it's so widespread, and it's affecting everybody."

Historically, women have been conditioned to laugh off, divert attention, and stay silent when they've been mistreated. This response was necessary for their survival because the alternative was shame, isolation, or punishment, since the chances were slim that a woman would be believed. Survivors who spoke up were labeled as troublemakers or untrustworthy; their reputation and ability to work elsewhere could be compromised; and they could be blacklisted, not only by their specific employers, but throughout an entire industry. And it would somehow all be their fault. These women would be mercilessly judged and coerced into leaving. This phenomenon is called *victim blaming*—a harmful and self-righteous move that both men (and women) can use to control the narrative. This conditioned response keeps the status quo (patriarchy) firmly in place.

Women have always been vulnerable when they speak out, since they risk not only ostracism, but the likelihood that they won't be believed. In fact, in a 2017 Harris Poll, only 20% surveyed thought they'd be supported if they spoke up.[59]

Today women are learning to join forces. When they unify their response to #MeToo behaviors, they won't be as easily dismissed or ignored. For example, here's what happened at Nike headquarters in

---

59   Mikaela Kiner, "What HR Needs To Do in the Wake of #MeToo," *Seattle Business* magazine, August 14, 2018, https://www.seattlebusinessmag.com/commentary/what-hr-needs-do-wake-metoo.

March 2018 when repeated complaints by women to HR about sexual harassment were met with inaction and were repeatedly ignored: The women created their own grassroots survey asking female colleagues whether they had experienced harassment and discrimination.[60] The results of the survey and the women's complaints made it to the desk of CEO Mark Parker. Women joining together led to a series of internal investigations that resulted in the firing and resignations of approximately a dozen senior leaders.[61]

The Politics of #MeToo and the Election of Donald Trump

How did we arrive at #MeToo? Fran Dunaway has a theory on why #MeToo has taken hold.

FRAN DUNAWAY SAYS:
When Hillary lost and this ******bag got into office, it kind of paved the way. It showed the misogyny that is so the undercurrent in everything. We're just sick of it. I sobbed on the floor the night of the election. I thought, *Oh my god, this country hates women. It's really that bad.*

---

60 Alexia Fernández Campbell, "Report: Human Resource Managers at Nike Ignored Complaints from Women Employees for Years," *Vox*, April 30, 2018, https://www.vox.com/policy-and-politics/2018/4/30/17302130/nike-women-harassment-discrimination-survey.

61 "Five More Executives Fired as Nike Confronts Workplace Harassment," France 24, May 10, 2018, https://www.france24.com/en/20180510-executives-fired-nike-confronts-workplace-harassment.

My mom told me she had the exact same response. Trump's election played an undeniable role in the rise of #MeToo. After hearing him speak off-the-record to *Access Hollywood* host Billy Bush, many became outraged. Trump described how he prepared for an interview with a female reporter, saying, "I better use some Tic Tacs just in case I start kissing her. You know, I'm automatically attracted to beautiful—I just start kissing them. It's like a magnet. Just kiss. I don't even wait. And when you're a star, they let you do it. You can do anything. . . . Grab 'em by the pussy. You can do anything."[62] Many people thought these comments would seal Trump's fate. Sadly, much of the country, including 53% of white women voters, did not see these comments as incongruous with someone capable and deserving of leading our country and dictating their rights as women.[63]

Trump's words displayed how power and entitlement enable this kind of behavior, and reinforce that as a society, many believe it's not that big a deal if men speak about women as objects and use women as the targets of their advances. Trump's words were dismissed (including by his wife) as "locker room talk," "men being men," and "boys being boys." We need to listen closely when people make these kinds of excuses and refuse to hold men to a reasonable standard. At work, sexist remarks are often dismissed by people by saying, "Oh, that's just so-and-so." This is code for an unwillingness to hold that person accountable. Accepting that norm means allowing men to dehumanize and dominate women. Not anymore!

Fran says, "I don't believe people are intentional about this either.

---

62   "Transcript: Donald Trump's Taped Comments About Women," *The New York Times*, accessed October 27, 2018, https://www.nytimes.com/2016/10/08/us/donald-trump-tape-transcript.html.

63   Anthony Zurcher, "Reality Check: Who Voted for Donald Trump?," November 9, 2016, US Election 2016 section, https://www.bbc.com/news/election-us-2016-37922587.

They just haven't examined what they believe, or what their thoughts are, or how they react, until they're confronted." Her assessment explains why Americans voted Trump into office. His tough-guy demeanor and refusal to show regret was interpreted by some as a sign of strength, rather than dysfunction. His ability to get away with bad behavior no matter how outrageous said to certain voters that he could fearlessly lead our country. His sexist actions of the past weren't seen as #MeToo examples: They were dismissed because his money and power somehow meant he could behave however he wished. Donald Trump is the poster child for being treated as if he's beyond reproach. There really isn't a better example of white, male privilege.

Who's the Victim Here? + the Pence Effect

Men who are accused of assault and discrimination are often given more sympathy than their victims. Kate Manne, the author of *Down Girl: The Logic of Misogyny*, helps us understand why. She coined the term *himpathy* to describe a typical response people have toward men when sexual allegations are made against them. Himpathy is a phenomenon where the perpetrator in power will be coddled. His colleagues, peers, family, and the public will feel terrible for the stress the accusations have caused him. The attack on his reputation will be seen as violent, and far worse than what his victim experienced. Just think about how backward that is. We saw this demonstrated in the hearings for Justice Brett Kavanaugh. His allies were appalled that his reputation was sullied, his livelihood was impacted, and he was required to wait ten extra days before confirmation to the Supreme Court.

On the flip side, Dr. Christine Blasey Ford had endured decades of emotional distress, then received death threats against herself and her family when her story was made public. Her allegations of being assaulted by Kavanaugh when they both were teenagers were supported by clear recollections of the moment and the lasting impact this attack had on her. Yet few were surprised when those allegations were dismissed. Fast-forward to Kavanaugh's confirmation hearing, which was a veritable repeat of the Clarence Thomas hearings when Anita Hill accused Thomas of sexual harassment in 1991.

Anita Hill was the victim of harassment, not the perpetrator. Still, she was asked the following questions by the all-white-male Senate Judiciary Committee:

- Are you a scorned woman?

- Are you a zealot civil rights believer that progress will be turned back, if Clarence Thomas goes on the court?

- Do you have a martyr complex?[64]

Both Blasey Ford and Hill were asked why they didn't raise allegations earlier, even though it's common for victims of assault and abuse to wait years before reporting incidents.[65] Both were subjected to character assassination and death threats. In both cases, the hearings and those presiding over them favored speed over depth. Women marveled at Blasey Ford's courage because we know what happens when women dare to challenge power and privilege. The survivors, not the perpetrators, are the ones who are threatened, blacklisted, and driven away from their jobs while the harassers benefit from *himpunity*—a habit we have of letting men off the hook particularly for harmful actions committed against women.

After Justice Kavanaugh's confirmation, Trump declared it was

---

64 https://www.cbsnews.com/news/here-are-some-of-the-questions-anita-hill-fielded-in-1991/

65 https://www.chicagotribune.com/news/opinion/commentary/ct-perspec-victim-sexual-assault-reluctance-to-report-brett-kavanaugh-0926-story.html

"a very scary time for young men in America."[66] Lynzy Lab Stewart responded to that comment by capturing the collective reaction of women everywhere. Her viral video features her singing "Scary Time for Boys."[67] Stewart's lyrics contrast the precautions women have become so accustomed to (not walking alone at night, jogging with headphones on, or living in a ground-floor apartment) with Trump's fear for men's well-being should they be held accountable for their behavior (a woman they've assaulted might turn up any time to report them, and they can't have sex without consent). A talented songwriter and musician with an eye for irony, using her voice and ukulele Stewart shines a light on the hypocrisy of worrying about men facing consequences for assault and harassment versus the lack of safety that impedes women's everyday lives.[68]

A possible unintended consequence of the #MeToo movement is that men will avoid one-on-one meetings with women and will exclude women from key events such as dinner meetings and travel opportunities. This sexist behavior has been named the *Pence effect*, after Vice President Mike Pence, who publicly stated that he refuses to dine alone with any woman other than his wife and won't attend any function where alcohol is served without his wife. This kind of thinking can lead to huge setbacks for women.[69] Unless men also choose not to

---

66 Jeremy Diamond, "Trump Says It's 'a Very Scary Time for Young Men in America,'" *CNN*, October 2, 2018, https://www.cnn.com/2018/10/02/politics/trump-scary-time-for-young-men-metoo/index.html.

67 https://www.youtube.com/watch?v=N34hehRgw9g

68 Lynzy Lab, *A Scary Time*, accessed December 14, 2018, https://www.youtube.com/watch?v=N34hehRgw9g.

69 Gillian Tan and Katia Porzecanski, "Wall Street Rule for the #MeToo Era: Avoid Women at All Cost," Bloomberg News, December 3, 2018, https://www.bloomberg.com/news/articles/2018-12-03/a-wall-street-rule-for-the-metoo-era-avoid-women-at-all-cost.

meet privately with other men, this separate and unequal treatment for women may well constitute discrimination.

The Role of HR in the Wake of #MeToo

Teri Citterman asked a question I've been asking myself for a while: "If more women than men work in HR, why hasn't there been swifter action and less tolerance of harassment in the face of #MeToo?" Even the most savvy and well-intentioned HR professionals have found these concerns challenging to navigate. It's even harder when an HR leader is less experienced, when they report to an executive who's part of the problem, and when HR lacks executive support and sponsorship. Very often, the HR leader is the only woman on the leadership team, surrounded by powerful men, one of whom is her boss.

Stories like what happened to Uber employee Susan Fowler in 2017 do not portray HR departments favorably. Fowler was sexually propositioned via chat by her manager within weeks of starting the job. When she contacted HR, they gave her two options. She reported, "(i) I could either go and find another team and then never have to interact with this man again, or (ii) I could stay on the team, but I would have to understand that he would most likely give me a poor performance review when review time came around, and there was nothing they could do about that." She was later blocked when trying to transfer to another team, due to what Uber called "undocumented performance problems." Yet Fowler's *documented* performance reviews had all been perfect.[70]

As a woman in HR, I've been fortunate to spend much of my

---

70   Susan Fowler, "Reflecting on One Very, Very Strange Year at Uber," Susan Fowler (blog), February 19, 2017, https://www.susanjfowler.com/blog/2017/2/19/reflecting-on-one-very-strange-year-at-uber.

career at companies where leadership backed me 100% when I needed to investigate cases of harassment and discrimination, even when it meant terminating a man who was otherwise a top performer. I've also had to fight hard at times for what I believed to be the right outcome. There was one incident where the manager took nearly a week to decide whether an offense was egregious enough for termination. To me, there was no question. The employee had repeatedly propositioned multiple women, using grotesque language, in front of witnesses. When HR investigated, he didn't deny it. He merely said he was drunk at the time. If his boss recommended anything short of termination following the investigation, I wanted the CEO to hear about it. If the perpetrator didn't get fired, I realized that I could no longer work for this company. I was prepared to walk away if it turned out that the company was willing to tolerate behavior that was not only illegal and predatory, but completely against my personal values. Luckily, it didn't come to that. But not everyone in HR has the luxury or privilege to give up their livelihood. I'm not trying to defend HR professionals who do the wrong thing. I do want to point out that workplace issues are systemic, and one person alone (the HR leader) is not enough to change company culture and decision-making. HR needs to take allegations seriously and create a safe place for complainants to come forward, with support of the executive team.

Tet Salva talks about a corporate experience that still bothers her. "I was at a team offsite, when the senior vice president of sales came up behind me. He stepped in close and basically felt me up. But because he brought in a huge revenue stream for the company in the millions of dollars, even though I knew I had to do something, I also knew I had no fighting chance. But then again, maybe the system might listen, so I went to HR and told them what had happened. Out of fear of being construed as a liar, I offered, 'The hotel has cameras all over the place. You could probably get a video of it. I'm sure you want evidence, right?' I also told my boss, who happened to be a friend. She was very chummy with the guys and didn't seem to believe me. HR said, 'Sorry, our hands are tied because he says he couldn't recall anything like that happening.'"

Afterward, Tet said it was awful to be there—awful to be around him. She also sought the counsel of a lawyer, who told her, "Well, you're going to spend a lot of money trying to convince these people that he did it. Do you have the strength and energy to go through that? You'll probably spend more time and money on this, and he'll still have a job. You won't." That's when doubt kicked in. She wondered if she was to blame for what had happened. She started beating herself up for "attracting that kind of energy." This sparked years of doubt, shame, and anger. Her story is typical of many women.

> *"The company mindset that says, 'If you have an issue, go to HR' needs to change."*

TET SALVA SAYS:
"If I could turn back time, I would have called him out or made a bigger stink about it. I'd talk to his boss and bring it up further that the behavior was unacceptable. We no longer have to retract or get small. We have permission to say without hesitation, 'Hey, that was inappropriate. Don't do that.'"

The company mindset that says, "If you have an issue, go to HR" needs to change. Yes, HR plays a critical role in defining company culture and values, and it's the job of HR to ensure there's a confidential place to voice concerns. HR professionals must be responsive and objective. They need to take swift action when issues are raised and recommend appropriate consequences that cannot be influenced by the perpetrator's seniority or job performance. But it isn't feasible to rely on just one person or department as the keeper of culture. *All senior leaders must be held equally accountable and be part of the solution.* This is how we instill values and hold the company, customers, and vendors accountable when they're not appropriate or respectful. If the leadership team is a sexist boys' club, HR hardly has the power to change the culture; organizations emulate their leaders.

I want to address the suspicion that HR is "on the company's side." I'm confident that I speak for many HR professionals when I say yes, we are; but we also know it's in the company's best interest to create a safe and inclusive culture where everyone

> *"Why hasn't HR dropped everything to respond quickly, discreetly, and effectively to complaints of abuse and harassment?"*

is free from harassment and discrimination. It is never in the interest of the company to permit anyone to exclude, mistreat, or disenfranchise their colleagues.

As mentioned previously, a 2017 Harris Poll found that just 20% of women who were surveyed believed their company would support them if they spoke out.[71, 72] Why hasn't HR dropped everything to respond quickly, discreetly, and effectively to complaints of abuse and harassment? I believe that the combination of poorly defined HR responsibilities, a deficit of training, plus a lack of leadership accountability are to blame. HR has an imperative to act on,

---

71 https://theharrispoll.com/

72 https://www.seattlebusinessmag.com/commentary/what-hr-needs-do-wake-metoo

investigate, and fairly resolve complaints. They also need the tools, resources, and leadership support to fulfill those responsibilities.

What Happens When Leaders Are the Problem?

While HR has their imperative, all leaders are, at the same time, responsible for ensuring safe, productive places where employees can succeed. We need leaders who will implement anti-harassment policies and hold everyone accountable, including HR. A company's culture doesn't always align with its stated aspirations. Many successful companies treat employees respectfully. Others are toxic—meaning HR and/or senior leaders ignore or condone unacceptable behavior.

I've been fortunate to work mostly with leaders who don't tolerate harassment, discrimination, or abuse. When I knew a leader would support tough outcomes, even when it meant disciplining or terminating people who were otherwise "high performers," I've been free to act with integrity. What about companies where support is lacking, where so-called performance is valued above behavior? I've worked there too, and I can tell you those are hard places for an HR professional to stay without compromising their own values and integrity.

What happens when leaders are the problem? Imagine being a new or junior HR professional and raising concerns about the CEO. Boards, advisors, and venture firms can play more active roles by ensuring that everyone, including HR, has a safe, confidential way to report concerns. It's also undeniable that some HR people lack capability to navigate and investigate certain kinds of complaints. That's not to say they're incompetent, but have they been trained? What tools do they have to act on employee concerns, conduct proper investigations, and remedy complex interpersonal issues? Leaders are responsible for ensuring that all employees, including HR professionals, have the resources they need to perform their roles effectively.

What leaves me heartsick are cases where employees courageously share their concerns to no avail. As someone who cares about women, respectful workplaces, fairness, and transparency, I've been grappling with the causes and consequences of HR's failure to act on even the most egregious cases of harassment and abuse. According to Workforce, a publication focused on the intersection of people management and business strategy, "Victims accuse HR of failing to adequately deal with complaints of improper or illegal behavior, provide proper reporting channels, or take other actions as warranted."[73]

Whatever barriers they face, I hope my HR colleagues use their resources to navigate difficult situations. For me, as a person who cares about women, fairness, and transparency, recent events highlight the need to educate all leaders and redouble our efforts if we're going to have healthy, inclusive workplaces where women can work without fear of harassment and abuse.

Claiming "Confusion" Is Actually a Form of Resistance

Are women's demands in the wake of #MeToo really that confusing? They are not. One way to understand the knee-jerk reaction of some men is to remember that claiming they are confused is just a form of defiance or intransigence. Anyone who suggests that the rules of workplace interaction are suddenly gray, or that it's now unclear what men can say or do in a professional setting, is resisting the need to change. It may be unconscious, but this type of resistance is still harmful.

Cheryl mentions working for an arena football team early in her career. "The sexism was atrocious. As the only woman trainer, I got my ass slapped and heard all the dirty, nasty things that men would say. I grew up in sports, so I blew it off and didn't think much about

---

73   https://www.workforce.com/2018/04/03/hr-responds-metoo-movement-2/

it. And because I didn't have allies in that space, I just said, 'Whatever.' That's been the coping mechanism of many women. Some even prided themselves on their ability to 'let it go' at their own expense."

Cheryl continues, "Now, when I see sexual harassment, it triggers something in me because I've suppressed it for so long. If I were back in that setting today, I'd rip those men a new asshole. I wouldn't hesitate to really tear into someone and report it, write about it, and educate other women and men about why it's not OK for you to do that to someone."

A friend shared an embarrassing incident with me. When she was seated between two male colleagues, one leaned behind her back and said to the other, "I bet I could take off her bra in three seconds." My friend was mortified, not only by what he said, but by who might have heard. She couldn't recall exactly how she responded, but she remembers making a joke or saying something to move the conversation along. It kept her from sleeping that night. Like so many women, she internalized it and blamed herself for laughing and not knowing what to say.

Another friend heard a woman who was in charge of training in the construction industry speak about dealing with harassment. She encouraged women employees not to complain about harassment and offensive comments, but also, not to laugh. She encouraged them to seek mentors and resolve things quietly. This kind of advice perpetuates the problem. It keeps the burden to change and transcend the issues on women, versus putting the responsibility on men and business owners to create spaces where people are required to treat each other with respect.

MALA SINGH SAYS:
"I think every working woman has had some kind of #MeToo experience. When I was younger, I worked at a hospital. There was a man who'd stop what he was doing to stare me up and down with a smirk on his face. This happened every single time I walked past him. This changed how I acted at work and the way I dressed. At all times, I had to think about where I was going and where he might be. That's not something any person should have to endure."

Heather Lewis recalls a man at work who repeatedly made both public and private remarks about her looks.

HEATHER LEWIS SAYS:
"It didn't matter what I was wearing, he would often have something to say about my dress that day, or how my heels did wonders for my butt. I was the only female in the room and the youngest person by about fifteen years, and there was never a time where anybody said, 'You're a sixty-something-year-old man in a position of power. She's in her twenties. Your comments are entirely inappropriate!'"

Like many women, Heather didn't see the use in pushing back. "At the time, my employer was experiencing financial difficulties. I didn't feel confident that my job would be secure, should the issue be escalated to leadership. The man making these comments was influential and had gotten away with this kind of behavior before. I worried I would be perceived as the problem."

Fran has her share of unpleasant memories that range from being molested by a family friend at age fourteen to one professor in college who chased her around his desk, and another who graded her papers in red ink, adding hearts and arrows.

FRAN DUNAWAY SAYS:

"At age fourteen, I felt guilty—like there was no one I could tell. I was very much deferential to male privilege, even though my mother is a strong, outspoken woman. Her deference was to the male gender. There was just nowhere to go."

Heather talks about wanting to protect her daughter.

"Becoming a parent was a big piece in cementing the bond between me and everybody else who's experienced #MeToo. This shouldn't be happening to any of us, and I feel a strong sense of responsibility."

As a mother, I also feel motivated to effect change because I do not want this happening when my kids enter the workplace. I don't want them to suffer the same kind of bias, stereotyping, or harm that so many people have endured. That goes for both my son and my

"We must talk with boys about their privilege, so they can grow up as advocates."

daughter. We must talk with boys about their privilege, so they can grow up as advocates. I want my son Simon to be a proud *feminist*, to promote equality, and to grow up knowing girls and women are as capable as men; that they deserve equal respect, as well as the same professional and financial opportunities. I want him to be someone who prevents further victimization of women and who understands what justice looks like.

How Do #MeToo Perpetrators Make Amends?

This leads us to another pressing question: How do #MeToo perpetrators properly make amends? Can they? Opinions on this question vary. It's almost easier to name what forms of punishment and redemption aren't acceptable. For instance, nine months after Louis C.K. admitted to exposing his penis and masturbating in front of women without their consent, he made a surprise, fifteen-minute appearance in front of a crowd who gave him a standing ovation at New York's Comedy Cellar. While some patrons applauded, others walked out, offended that he made no reference or apology following the allegations.[74]

Feminist leader Roxane Gay answers this question brilliantly in *The New York Times*. "How long should a man like Louis C.K. pay for what he did?" She writes, "He should pay until he demonstrates some measure of understanding of what he has done wrong and the extent of the harm he has caused. He should attempt to financially compensate his victims for all the work they did not get to do because of his efforts to silence them. He should facilitate their getting the professional opportunities they should have been able to take advantage of

---

74 Roxane Gay, "Opinion | Louis C.K. and Men Who Think Justice Takes as Long as They Want It To," *The New York Times*, August 29, 2018, https://www.nytimes.com/2018/08/29/opinion/louis-ck-comeback-justice.html.

all these years. He should finance their mental health care as long as they may need it. He should donate to nonprofit organizations that work with sexual harassment and assault victims. He should publicly admit what he did and why it was wrong without excuses and legalese and deflection. Every perpetrator of sexual harassment and violence should follow suit."[75]

Let's look now at what each of us can do to stand up and promote safety, equality, advocacy, and accountability at work.

TERI CITTERMAN SAYS:
"It doesn't matter what your looks are, you're going to get hit on. It's important to be prepared. You can't say nothing."

WHAT EACH OF US CAN DO

1. Trust Your Instincts and Share Your Stories

Kristina Bergman, CEO and founder of Integris Software, has been leading change for women in the tech sector. She spoke at our recent Seattle Human Resources Meetup and made an unforgettable comment. She said women have a "Spidey sense," meaning that they can recognize creepy guys a mile away. In the San Francisco area, there is literally

---

75   Gay, "Louis C.K. and Men Who Think Justice Takes as Long as They Want It To."

a Slack channel[76] where women warn each other who to avoid. When inappropriate things happen, it's easy to second-guess what you just heard, felt, or saw. Being able to share concerns with other women helps targets of predatory behavior check out their intuition, gain validation, and offer support to others.[77]

Fran illustrates how other women can verify sexual inappropriateness. She mentions a male venture capitalist, a partner of the firm, who crossed the line in a business setting. Fran says, "There was a twenty-five-year-old woman bending over to put something on the table, and this guy, who was old enough to be her grandfather, said how good she looked bending over the table. My eyebrow shot up. At first, I wasn't positive of what I heard, but it shook me, which rattled my confidence."

Notice how our default is *not* to trust what we heard or saw. Luckily, Fran said, "Screw it." To show her support, she contacted the young woman through her email listed on LinkedIn. She didn't want to use the woman's company email, in case that would put her in an awkward position. The woman replied with thanks, saying she had reported it and it was being handled internally. This was a solid example of women's advocacy—how women can let each other know what they see and whose side they're on.

---

76 Slack is messaging communications tool often used in technology companies, where information is organized in channels. Slack can also be set up for informal groups or friends from different companies.

77 Kristina Bergman, "Nike. Uber. Weinstein. What HR Needs in the Wake of #MeToo," panel discussion, August 8, 2018.

2. Practice What You'll Say and Be Prepared

Teri Citterman mentors women to help them see when sexual advances and unproductive flirting might be getting in the way of business. She says, "It doesn't matter what your looks are, you're going to get hit on. It's important to be prepared. You can't say nothing." Because it's happened repeatedly to her, Teri has learned how to spot the signals and respond. At first, she admits being vicious with her replies. Even though anger and aggression are natural, that's not the way Teri wants to handle things today. "I think grace is a much better way. You have to practice for that."

A man who was introduced to Teri at a large technology company said, "The only reason these guys are helping you is because you're hot."

Another man told Teri, "If we didn't work together, I'd want to fuck you right now."

Her response was brilliant: "You know what? I'm going to let you take that back. You have twenty seconds."

He asked, "Oh, I shouldn't have said that, should I?"

"Yeah, you shouldn't have said that," Teri replied. Grace over aggression is her mission, although sometimes, she jokes, the response is more like "I can't believe you just fucking said that!" Once again, it's better to speak up imperfectly than to sit in silence.

Emelia Holden, a twenty-one-year-old waitress, didn't hesitate to take matters into her own hands when a man groped her during her shift at Vinnie Van Go-Go's in Savannah, Georgia. *People* magazine reported, "In surveillance footage of the incident, 31 year-old Ryan Cherwinski is shown grabbing Holden's backside as he walks behind her. Holden immediately turns around, and grabs him by his collar and slams him into a counter. 'I looked at him and I said, "You don't touch me, motherf*****!"' Holden said, "'I didn't even think, I just reacted. I don't know how I reacted the way I did. I've never done that before.'"[78]

Remember the older gentleman who would incessantly comment on Heather's appearance? Heather wishes she could go back and properly address the situation today. What would she say if it happened again? Her choice in words is nearly flawless: "You know what? I'm sorry this is still happening. I didn't say anything last time around, but I'm going to say something now because your behavior has an impact on everyone in this room. The kind of leadership that you're demonstrating right now is toxic. I have a responsibility to the women who are younger than me; and frankly, I have a responsibility to the men in this room who have said nothing, to let you know that your behavior isn't okay, and it needs to stop."

Business leaders who witness abusive comments want and expect confrontation to come from HR. But actually, it's *their* participation that we need most. As a junior employee, Heather shouldn't have been the one to defend herself. Leadership must step in—even if they won't step in

> *"Remember, everyone can do something. At this time in our history, it is even more important that we show up for one another as active bystanders."*

---

78 Char Adams, "Georgia Waitress, 21, Who Body-Slammed Man After He Groped Her in Pizzeria Speaks Out," *People*, July 19, 2018, https://people.com/human-interest/emelia-holden-body-slam-georgia-pizzeria/.

because it's the right thing to do, they should step in to protect the company's bottom line. Costs of litigation are high, and a #MeToo incident can affect recruitment, retention, and create a hostile and unproductive work environment.

3. Intervene as a Bystander and Learn How to Become an Upstander

Being targeted with harassment because of your race, sex, religion, color, gender, size, orientation, ability, age, or origin is a horrific experience. If you're surrounded by bystanders who see what is happening and choose to do nothing, it's even more devastating. It doesn't have to be that way. *Bystanders* become *upstanders* when they learn to recognize unwanted behavior at work, speak up on behalf of others, and take action.

Hollaback! provides digital training on how to do your part to protect your colleagues.[79] They say, "Remember, everyone can do something. At this time in our history, it is even more important that we show up for one another as active bystanders. Research shows that even a knowing glance can significantly reduce trauma for the person who is targeted. One of the most important things we can do is to let the person who is targeted know, in some way, however big or small, that they are not alone."[80]

Remember, victims may laugh when they are put in an

---

79   Hollaback! is a global, people-powered movement to end harassment by working together to understand the problem, ignite public conversations, and develop innovative strategies that ensure equal access to public spaces; https://www.ihollaback.org.

80   "Bystander Intervention Resources | Hollaback! End Harassment," Hollaback! Together We Have the Power to End Harassment (blog), accessed December 8, 2018, https://www.ihollaback.org/resources/bystander-resources/.

uncomfortable situation. That's because they are unsure how to respond. People may laugh along at inappropriate jokes and comments because they don't want to call attention to themselves or isolate themselves from the group. That does not mean they are comfortable or appreciate what's happening. As a bystander, you can reach out to people who were targets of unwanted remarks and ask them privately if they were offended. This is where you get to choose to be part of the solution.

4. Ask for an Ombuds

An ombuds is defined as a representative. It's a term often used in the workplace to describe an objective, neutral person who employees can approach with their concerns and complaints. The job of the ombuds is to objectively listen to issues and guide employees. If your company has an HR and/or diversity function, members of those teams are often the ones who will field complaints. Some companies have a confidential telephone hotline that employees can use.

Small companies that don't have an HR function are asking where complaints should go. There are new businesses springing up, like tEQuitable, which describes itself as a digital ombuds. Similarly, AllVoices helps employees anonymously report harassment. Bravely offers workers a third-party, independent trained coach they can call to sound out conflicts or communication problems. All of these are efforts to fill the "trust gap" between employees, managers, and the human resources department. They are answers to a need for workplace respect and safety, and they ultimately serve to stop abuses of power.

5. Fix Things from Within

Company leaders are re-examining traditional anti-harassment training. They're rewriting policies and adding repercussions, but we should look at the stats. Even in the wake of #MeToo, "only 10% of 1,512 adults working in the United States said their organizations added more anti-sexual harassment training or resources."[81] One type of training alone cannot change behavior and effect lasting change. We need advocacy training, bystander training, unconscious bias training—a series of ongoing programs and other learning experiences. Executives must act as role models—leading hard conversations about harassment, discrimination, respect, and values—and actively advocate for inclusion. They need to be willing to discipline or terminate high performers and high-ranking individuals who perpetuate and tolerate harmful and illegal behaviors.

Reuters gave a tremendous review to Kristina Bergman, founder and CEO of Integris, when she made the unusual decision to include an anti-sexual harassment clause in her company's voting agreement with investors. Kristina wanted a culture of inclusion and respect supported by board members who shared those values. "The clause calls for an investigation should any board director be accused of sexual harassment. If it is found that there was 'reasonable probability' that an incident occurred, the director would be removed." To Kristina's

---

81 Kathy Gurchiek, "Sexual Harassment Prevention Training Should Involve Real Conversations," SHRM, May 30, 2018, https://www.shrm.org/resourcesandtools/ hr-topics/behavioral-competencies/global-and-cultural-effectiveness/pages/sexual-harassment-prevention-training-should-involve-real-conversations.aspx.

knowledge, she is the only founder to date who has developed a "removal and replacement" clause like this.[82]

Ruchika reports how her colleague was sexually harassed by her male boss on a business trip. The organization promptly fired him. Even though Ruchika had other negative experiences in that company, she said the swift action they took made her feel much more comfortable. It gave her hope and demonstrated that the company leaders had their hearts in the right place.

There's No Turning Back

When #MeToo erupted like a volcano, it was a long-overdue reaction to decades of oppression and harassment that women have suffered silently. Inappropriate behavior, harassment, and assault that had long been accepted as the status quo were finally being called out. Perpetrators were named publicly and held to account. By joining forces, women found the courage and support to speak up publicly, often about incidents that had happened long ago. In doing so, they provided language and became role models for the next generation. Seeing women reclaim their stories in this way was nothing short of inspiring. We're addressing issues that have always been risky and difficult to talk about out loud, and yet there's no turning back. Discussing this kind of mistreatment and working to prevent it in the future can be more energizing than we ever thought possible. I hope that, like me, you feel more informed and empowered after hearing these stories.

---

82   Salvador Rodriguez, "U.S. Tech Startups Fight Sexual Harassment with Tougher Policies," Reuters, July 12, 2017, https://www.reuters.com/article/startups-sexualdiscrimination/u-s-tech-startups-fight-sexual-harassment-with-tougher-policies-idUSL1N1K32DS.

END-OF-CHAPTER CHECKLIST: #METOO

Mid-Career and Next Gen Women:

☐ Trust yourself. If something makes you feel uncomfortable, don't write it off.

☐ Confide in a trusted friend, mentor, coach, or therapist. Sharing your story can be cathartic and give you a much-needed sounding board.

☐ It's an unfortunate reality, but you should practice and prepare to speak up for yourself. Having a ready response like Teri's, "I'll give you twenty seconds to take that back," makes it easier so you don't have to think on your feet.

☐ Review the channels that are available to you at work to confidentially report concerns. If it's not apparent where to go, ask HR, your manager, or your supervisor.

☐ Report inappropriate comments and behavior. It's not up to you to prove what happened. The burden is on the company to investigate and resolve issues.

Male Advocates:

☐ Tell women that you're an advocate. It helps to know who's sympathetic and whom they can trust.

☐   Call out other men. If they are being inappropriate, regardless of whether it's "just a joke," remind them that it doesn't belong at work (or anywhere else). It's so much easier for men to do this with other men.

☐   Thank women for coming forward with their stories and concerns. It is not an easy thing to do. They're risking a lot by opening up, so recognize and honor that.

HR, DEI, and Other Business Leaders:

☐   Make sure there are multiple ways for people to share complaints and concerns. Communicate these channels in your handbook, on your intranet, and at company and team meetings, so people know where to go.

☐   What gets measured gets done. Recognize and reward women and men who champion, mentor, and create opportunities for women employees.

☐   Set aside time and money for diversity, equity, inclusion, and unconscious bias training supported by ongoing dialogue and refresher sessions. Make sure your managers are aware of their obligations if they witness or hear about inappropriate behavior.

16

SEND THE ELEVATOR BACK DOWN!

So far, we've explored how the impact and consequences of privilege and abuse of power deter and derail us at work and how women can join together to influence change. I've deliberately provided positive stories about women helping each other, yet there's a difficult reality we cannot ignore. The fact is, women aren't always united. Women can be unnecessarily competitive with one another, for no reason, when it serves no purpose. Female rivalries can be brutal, and they must be addressed. Women need to work together if we want to dispel the myth that there's room for only one woman at the table. We must get on the same side, in order to create room and opportunities for more women to lead.

I want to be clear regarding my belief in and support of healthy competition. I am not suggesting that women cannot or should not compete with each other. What's important is that we compete without perpetuating the belief that there's only one seat at the table for women. That we compete without personal judgment, shaming, and stereotyping. That while competing to win, we must put at least as much if not more energy into helping all women rise.

To do this, we cannot ignore our own *internalized sexism* and allow it to hold other women back. Yes—even women can and do internalize messages that women are not as strong, competent, and capable as men. Women unconsciously integrate society's beliefs about their rightful place, and those messages can and do show up in how women judge other women. "*Internalized sexism* is the involuntary internalization by women of the sexist messages that are present in their societies and culture." Women can unknowingly "reinforce sexism by utilizing and relaying sexist messages that they've internalized."[83] "When we compete with other women at work, collapse after being shamed for our choices by another woman, or abuse our own power over another woman, we are colluding with a sexist culture."[84]

By asking women to collaborate, stand up, and speak up for one another, I don't believe I'm holding women to a higher standard than men. I'm asking women to find opportunities for lasting change that will benefit all women. In his *WorkLife* podcast, Adam Grant presents an alternative take on rivalry; what he describes as supportive rivalry. Grant describes how rivalry makes us better, when we compete *with* collaboration. It may not surprise you that being in direct competition with an accomplished rival increases your focus and motivation to fight harder and do better. Grant tells the story of how in the 2016 Olympic trials, finalist Shalane Flanagan slowed down to help her rival and training partner, Amy Cragg. Grant sets the stage by explaining, "It's supposed to be every runner for herself. And only the winners get the big sponsorship dollars. So why did Shalane give up her advantage to help her opponent win? And should you ever do that?" When Cragg's pain began to slow her down at mile 13 of 26, Flanagan slowed down too, feeling they should stick together. Since this is history, I can tell you without a spoiler alert that Cragg wound up winning.

It happened that I was listening to this very podcast on my way to a gathering of women business leaders. It dawned on me that three of

---

83   https://finallyfeminism101.wordpress.com/2007/10/20/internalized-sexism/

84   https://www.ellevatenetwork.com/articles/7445-5-ways-misogyny-has-worked-its-way-into-the-lives-of-women

us who were there—myself, Lora Poepping, who runs Plum Coaching and Consulting, and Laura Doehle, who is the president of Resourceful—have created our own version of collaborative competition. We all do HR consulting, but each with a slightly different approach and target customer. Over the years we've chosen to focus on what's unique about our work versus where we overlap. By doing that, we've all found it much more advantageous (and fun!) to collaborate. For instance, Lora from Plum offered to lend me a consultant from her team when I was short on resources. And I referred a client to Laura at Resourceful when I didn't have someone with the right background to meet the client's needs. Ours is just one example of how women can support their rivals. I'm sure there are many others.

For the sake of women's well-being and progress, we need to face how we're throwing ourselves and each other under the bus. We have to dig deep and explore why marriage, parenting, looks, and work have become such great sources of insecurity, leading women to judge one another. Women must get curious and ask themselves, "How can I do better for myself and all women?"

When I asked about women treating each other badly, it resonated with the interviewees more than I expected. They reported having devastating interactions with female peers, managers, and even with HR (a profession that is more than 70% female,[85] and whose responsibility it to treat people with respect, to hear and investigate their concerns), including being judged and being made to feel ashamed. This type of treatment reinforces power standards and stereotypes that have dogged women since the beginning of time. Enough is enough. Women still create barriers for other women, often in the form of hazing, arbitrarily high standards, moving targets, and perpetuating the "one seat at the table" mentality. Both Christy and Heather experienced their women

---

85   recruitingheadlines.com/71-percent-of-hr-professionals-are-female/

bosses competing against them rather than welcoming them as contributing members of the team. I faced similar challenges with some, though not all, of my female bosses—one who told me not to speak in meetings, one who told me my job as a senior person was to work independently but then accused me of excluding her because I didn't ask her to join me in meetings, and one who repeatedly scolded me for keeping her in the dark even when I had her approval in writing. Truth is, there's much more at play when women perpetuate issues of sexism at work.

Women Are Still Being Stereotyped

Social conditioning is a problem. It defines how women are supposed to look, feel, and contribute to the world. We have to keep examining what we've been taught, what beliefs we've internalized, and how we can change outdated norms. Many of us grew up with Disney, which is questionable in its portrayal of women—beginning with women as princesses/damsels in distress.

When Snow White sang, "Someday My Prince Will Come," girls got the message that finding a husband is a primary goal in life, and that men have the power to complete you. Same with poor Cinderella and her mean stepmother and stepsisters. They locked her in a basement and forced her to clean and wear rags as clothing. All this so she wouldn't become the "one" to win the prince's love. As if love is something you can win! Wait, isn't that what happens on *The Bachelor*?

These messages set up a competitive environment that girls can't help but internalize from day one. That environment was rooted in the reality of an earlier time—when women were dependent on men for their livelihood, and had few or no rights to education, voting, or high-paying jobs. Later generations of girls benefited from Disney's evolution and willingness to reflect changing social structures, though these changes were long overdue. "The princesses in this era, specifically from 1989 to 2010, can be seen as rebellious and ambitious because they seek their own freedom, but they still get some sort-of happily ever after."[86]

I have a few real-life scenarios to back up the female rivalry stereotype. It's unfortunate, but the only people who have been outwardly unfriendly and undermining since I started Reverb have been women. There have been only a few, but it has been so disappointing. Some men have been aloof or unhelpful to me, but only women have been malicious. In each case, it was due to competition that in their eyes seemed to overshadow respect or camaraderie.

One woman was not even a direct competitor, but she told a mutual client that I charged too much. She knew my fees were in line with others, but she tried to sabotage my success. Why did she do that? What purpose did that serve for her? Another sought to take credit for my business model, even though it was one I had considered launching a decade earlier. A third accused me of lacking integrity when I won a piece of business that used to be hers. Though the client contacted me out of the blue, she accused me of using personal connections to steal a happy client out from under her. We need to talk about how and why women compete unfairly and unnecessarily with one another, so we can stop ourselves before we take steps or make accusations that could sabotage another woman's career. It's also helpful to learn how to recognize and respond, if you're the object of another woman's rivalry. Again, there is nothing wrong with *healthy* competition, which happens between women and men every day.

The women I spoke to also mentioned a hazing effect that takes place between women of different generations. Rather than lending a helping hand to their female colleagues, some older women want to

---

86 http://scholars.indstate.edu/bitstream/handle/10484/12132/Barber_McKenzie_2015_ HT.pdf?sequence=1&isAllowed=y

make sure younger women have to fight just as hard as they did to earn their place. The tactics women use to oppress each other are the same tactics used by society to maintain control and power over women. These include perpetuating the myth that there's room for only one woman, and holding women to double standards, thereby making success unattainable. While these behaviors are real, I see far more positive examples than negative ones. I watch people advocating for women they admire, groups of people coming together and creating networks to help women peers and female founders, and celebrations like Leslie's Champion Awards that recognize and celebrate high-impact women and their *sponsors*, advocates, and allies.

Keeping Our Own Biases in Check

To keep my own bias in check, I recently took the IAT (Implicit Association Test) for both race and gender. My score showed minimal bias when it comes to race, but more with regard to gender. Turns out, I too have some unfair stereotypes about women that are deeply ingrained. This doesn't mean I'm not a passionate feminist, it means that I've internalized the negative messages about women that I've heard and seen all my life. Even though I don't consciously believe any of them, I have to be careful not to apply unfair expectations to myself and other women.

When my kids were small, I can see now that I felt judgmental toward stay-at-home moms. Because my upbringing revolved around the value of work and developing a professional identity, I found their choice puzzling. I didn't realize that judging other women's choices about work and childcare is a common form of bias. Working in technology, I've noticed that upon meeting young women who are highly technical, sometimes I still feel a fleeting moment of surprise. This is painful to admit, but it happens. I quickly remind myself that the socially awkward guy in grubby clothes is a dated, inaccurate engineering stereotype. These unwanted thoughts serve as a reminder that no matter how forward thinking you are, no one is immune to the messages that seep into our unconscious.

During one interview, Becky Hammon, the first female NBA coach, she spoke about how she knew with 100% certainty that women make excellent coaches. However, she'd only seen men coach male sports teams. She'd never seen a woman in that role, so it didn't even seem like a possibility to her. This kind of unconscious bias plagues all of us. When we can't see who we want to be, it increases feelings of doubt and impostor syndrome.

Defying stereotypes is the antidote: Following a national ad campaign against stereotyping women in technical careers, within one week, 50,000 women had posted pictures on Twitter tagged #ILookLikeAnEngineer.[87] They wanted to show the modern-day face of female engineers and engineering students. This was an uplifting way to validate women's participation in a male-dominated field.

Women at Work: Competition or Sisterhood?

I once had a female boss who told me to refrain from asking questions in meetings because it was derailing and signaled a lack of trust in my peers. I was appalled by her feedback. Because I was already interviewing outside of the company and had sensed she wasn't on my side, I purposefully stopped our conversation to ensure that I heard her correctly. "So, you're saying I should ask fewer questions in meetings? Even if the question is relevant? Even if I can't follow the

---

87   Kathryn Varn, "Woman Behind #ILookLikeAnEngineer Says Campaign Against Gender Stereotypes Is 'Long Overdue,'" December 21, 2017, Technology section, https://www.nytimes.com/2015/08/06/technology/hashtag-aims-to-break-gender-stereotypes-in-engineering.html.

conversation without an answer to the question?" Her answer was "yes" every time. I knew the next time we sat down together, I'd be resigning, and that is exactly what happened. How could I possibly work in an environment where I was discouraged from getting the information needed to do my job?

Christy Johnson says that unfortunately her worst boss ever was a woman. What made her so hard to work for? She didn't follow through when she said she would. In conversations and debates, she only wanted to hear evidence that confirmed her own opinion, showing she was inflexible and not open to feedback. During one-on-one meetings they had together, she would take nearly 100% of the airtime sharing her personal problems. This did not leave any time to talk about work, Christy's development, or her future with the company. Christy remembers, "She gave personal feedback that wasn't actionable, like saying 'I don't trust you.' Then when I would ask for specific things I had done so I could improve, she wouldn't name them." She ran personal errands during the day, leaving Christy to answer to the executives who needed her. Christy made excuses for her boss and tried to help out by joining meetings while her boss was on a shopping excursion, only to get yelled at when she returned to the office. It was a lose/lose situation.

CHRISTY JOHNSON SAYS:
"She gave personal feedback that wasn't actionable, like saying 'I don't trust you.' Then when I would ask for specific things I had done so I could improve, she wouldn't name them."

Christy has a sad story from another organization, where she was one of only four female VPs at the company. "I was the newest one to join, and I was pretty sure the other three women didn't like me. At an executive meeting, one of the women VPs shared her screen without realizing her email was still open. In plain view, I could see the women had been talking about me. It was one of those moments when I was like, 'OK. Verified!'" What did Christy do? She was lucky that one of her male peers stepped in. He approached her after the meeting and said he was going to talk to the others about what he'd seen. Grateful, Christy thanked him and still considers him an advocate to this day.

Leslie Feinzaig says she used to prefer to work with men because the women she worked for and with, in highly competitive industries, could be brutal. She describes how women jockeyed for power and superiority. "Among speakers and event coordinators, for example, there can be a sense of 'you're not good enough for my stage,' 'you're not special enough for my thing.' It's conveyed in signals that imply, 'I'm busier than you,' 'It has to be on my turf and my time.'" But since she started the FFA with a strong culture and values around women supporting one another, the women she works with today are collaborative and share her mission. Leslie's example proves the impact leaders like her can have when they choose to emphasize cooperation over competition with peers.

Mar speaks about women who undermined each other in academics. This was especially tough for her because she wasn't raised to be competitive, nor did she play any team sports. There's evidence that when girls play a sport, especially if they continue throughout their teen years, they're better equipped to compete in other facets of life. "Learning to own victory and survive defeat in sports is apparently good training for owning triumphs and surviving setbacks at work."[88] In her discipline, there were so few women that

---

[88] https://www.theatlantic.com/magazine/archive/2014/05/the-confidence-gap/359815/

women often had to fend for themselves. Mar explains, "I watched women take men more seriously by deferring to their opinions in meetings or choosing men for important speaking engagements. As women, many of us had internalized misogyny—it was in the air we breathed. People were far more critical of females—dismissing their research questions as 'lightweight' or gossiping about the 'neurotic' behaviors of female faculty. Most women had to be twice as good as men to achieve tenure. At one school, no woman had ever even achieved tenure when I started. At another, I was the sole female in my department. In a third school, the only woman who had achieved tenure in the history of the department had two doctorates—she had literally worked twice as hard as the men."

MAR BRETTMAN EXPLAINS:
"Most women had to be twice as good as men to achieve tenure."

Harvard Business Review reports, "Several studies have found that because women operate under a higher-resolution microscope than their male counterparts do, their mistakes and failures are scrutinized more carefully and punished more severely. People who are scrutinized more carefully will, in turn, be less likely to speak up in meetings, particularly if they feel no one has their back. However, when women fail to speak up, it is commonly assumed that they lack confidence in their ideas."[89]

This misogynistic behavior of women holding down other women

---

89 *Harvard Business Review*, https://hbr.org/2018/05/what-most-people-get-wrong-about-men-and-women.

has an academic name: the "Queen Bee" phenomenon. Senior-level women have been known to distance themselves from junior women, perhaps to be more accepted by their male peers. "As a study published in *The Leadership Quarterly* concludes, this is a *response* to inequality at the top, not the cause. Trying to separate oneself from a marginalized group is, sadly, a strategy that's frequently employed."[90]

Tet Salva says that one of the biggest challenges women face in the workplace today is building a sisterhood, especially among female leaders. Indirect aggression among women is all too common. "We may not recognize it, but we play into gender stereotypes at work, and when a woman strays from the typical gender norm, for example, she becomes more assertive or takes charge, other women may have a hard time accepting it."

> *"Senior-level women have been known to distance themselves from junior women, perhaps to be more accepted by their male peers."*

Teri Citterman says some women leaders have been unsupportive because they told her to be less aggressive, even though her style was effective with clients. Their discomfort with her self-confidence said more about their own fears and insecurities, than what Teri needed to do in order to be more effective. This is another example of why we need to educate ourselves about stereotypes, so that we can consciously resist them.

Cheryl Ingram describes women as her biggest champions *and* her most exhausting adversaries, particularly older white women. She explains, "White women often say indirectly, 'I've had to work hard to get here, I'm not giving you anything easily.'" She elaborates,

---

90   Anne Welsh McNulty, "Don't Underestimate the Power of Women Supporting Each Other at Work," *Harvard Business Review*, September 3, 2018, https://hbr.org/2018/09/dont-underestimate-the-power-of-women-supporting-each-other-at-work.

as a woman of color, how some white women clients have unfairly interacted with her:

- **Talking to her like she's a child:** People, especially White men and women, tend to explain to me basic concepts in DEI like we're in kindergarten! They immediately assume that I only think diversity is about race and feel the need to lecture me on how they are not included in diversity. I also find that people will explain the basics of business to me, like how to write a contract, and why I need a CPA, etc. before they even realize or take the time to ask if I have these things in place. It is insulting and annoying.

- **Asking her to change her presentations:** I have had people ask for my content ahead of time and put things in and change it right before my presentation without even asking. I had a school administrator who used to treat me like I was the Black facilitator there to represent his belief in DEI and would micromanage my content. I later found out that he wanted to do this work. I also have had numerous companies try to change my content and make it superficial. It's like they want to use my face for the purpose of credibility but not my expertise.

- **Stereotyping her as an angry Black woman:** I was once in a meeting with a group of colleagues. There were two White women in the room who kept interrupting the women of Color but never interrupted the men. When I pointed out that it was happening, the White women in the room stopped, but it went to the next extreme. Immediately following my pointing out of the interruptions, they started holding their hands against their chest before they spoke as if to ward off an attacker. When I simply stated that "I notice that the two of you keep interrupting the women of Color but you're not interrupting the men." I remember her responding with "well my intention is not to hurt anyone's feelings." When I was pointing out the inequity, not the emotion, I even had a White female colleague say, "well in business I think it is OK to interrupt one another." But no one would recognize that this was happening.

- **Vetting her work twice as much as others:** I usually have to go through three to four interviews with a company and sometimes four to five calls in order to get them to purchase our services, even if they approached us. Companies on average have asked me for the following:

  - A case study of our work

  - A copy of our curriculum

  - A resume of all our employees

  - References from clients

  - To sit in on other trainings with other companies before they decide if they want to sign a contract or not

  - To drop our prices substantially by almost 40%

  - My firstborn! (joking)

  It's like they don't even think about the fact that most of our material is confidential. It's like they want our work for free before they pay for it! I get that it's the sales funnel, but this funnel seems like it has cracks in it.[91]

- **Displaying suspicion and a lack of trust:** I've been accused of overbilling a client who needed to meet every week but didn't want to pay us for the meetings. She felt like our meetings sometimes

---

91 As a consultant who offers training, thought not in the DEI space, I can attest that asking for one or two of these things is a typical vetting process. But asking for all and asking her to perform work for free, like sitting in on training without pay before they hire her, is unconscionable.

an hour or more should've been free. I have had clients who will want to meet with me daily to double-check our work. To be fair, some of it is because they have had terrible experiences with other consultants, but this leads to me having to suffer due to someone else's inability. That's where a lack of trust comes from, right, people having bad experiences? But most of the time it results in me being micromanaged and having to overcompensate for someone else's actions. This doesn't often work in our personal relationships or business.

- **Telling her how to do her job:** The worst was an older CEO of a nonprofit who was a very difficult woman. I couldn't tell her anything; she thought she knew everything! She used to be a consultant, not a DEI consultant, and sometimes other consultants are the worst clients. They always want to tell you how they would do it! Not to mention that her business was losing employees left and right and people were complaining about DEI. She felt she knew it all and they didn't need my help, but she hired me! She used to tell me how to ask DEI questions, and every time I made a recommendation, she would embellish what the organization had done and why they didn't need DEI. It was a mess! It was a humbling experience that caused me to walk away from my first executive and look for the signs of people who didn't really want my input, just my presence.

It's hard to develop strong bonds and collaborate if we are not clear on our biases. And many white women are still in the dark about their advantages and biases. They might be educated, but not in this arena. Cheryl explains, "White women have both privilege and oppression. White women have a privilege (race), which is not a fault but a fact. They also experience oppression as women versus white men who are dominant. No one should feel guilty for having a privilege because it's not a choice. They should ask how they can help others who don't share that privilege. White women still benefit from more opportunities than non-white women. According to the Women in the Workplace 2018 survey, "Women of color are not only significantly underrepresented, they are far less likely than others to be promoted to manager, more likely to face everyday discrimination and less likely to receive support from their managers."[92]

This is a hard message Cheryl often gives white women. It's even harder, she says, when they're liberals. Accepting that they too have hidden bias goes against their political beliefs of equality. Nonetheless, white women must become more open. They have to ask for and welcome the feedback from women of color. Do not defend or try to explain your intention. It takes emotional labor for women of color to confront their white peers and colleagues. They should be thanked for the risks they take to share their experiences which help others grow. This is not about comparative suffering, trying to rank one oppression over another. It is, however, critical that white women understand the facts, including where their experiences are similar to women of color, and where they diverge.

When I spoke to the Next Generation, women of color talked about older women in business who had accepted the status quo of a toxic, male-dominated environment. Next Gen women said that seasoned women (of all races) didn't seem to realize things could be different, nor did they feel motivated to discover their unconscious biases. Leslie urges accomplished women, "It's your responsibility to send the elevator back down or at least get out of the way." Don't let the fact that you've made it keep you from using your success to help others.

The younger women talked about being *gaslighted* by other women.

---

92 Women in the Workplace 2018 survey. https://www.mckinsey.com/featured-insights/gender-equality/women-in-the-workplace-2018

Gaslighting is a form of manipulation designed to make you think you're way off base or delusional. A person who gaslights might trivialize legitimate concerns, forget conversations, make themselves a victim, or deny promises they made. A friend told me about a gaslighting situation so extreme that she wound up resigning only two months into the job. In this case the boss was a man, but it's a good illustration of what gaslighting looks like.

Her boss, the CFO, had aggressively recruited her as head of people at a technology startup. One of her first goals was to organize anti-harassment and anti-discrimination training for the company. She researched a variety of solutions and chose a vendor who had impeccable references.

My friend ran her proposal by key executives then suggested they meet the vendor face to face. When she brought the final proposal to the CFO for approval, he went ballistic, berating my friend:

- How dare you make these arrangements without including me?

- Any other head of HR I know of would never make a recommendation like this without 100% backing of their boss.

- There's no way we're going to spend so much money and take people's valuable time for this kind of training. I don't see why you can't just stand up in front of the team and tell people how they can and can't behave. You're blowing this training way out of proportion.

- You're lucky I don't fire you on the spot.

When her shock subsided, my friend patiently reminded her boss of their earlier conversations. She reminded him that this training was a company priority that he had assigned her. She reminded him that if knowing the difference between right and wrong behavior was that easy, people would not behave the way they do. That managers needed a place to engage in conversations about what to do when they witness or suspect harassment, and so on. Eventually her boss calmed down and seemed to accept these arguments. He approved the training and participated grudgingly in the executive session. This was only one example of many where her boss gave urgent directives, changed his mind, gave and then withdrew approval, all without acknowledging that he was reprioritizing or changing course. Recognizing that it would be impossible to succeed in the face of such erratic behavior and constantly changing goals, she eventually fled that job for one where she could have real impact. It's not only men who are guilty of gaslighting; women do it too.

Why do some women try to get ahead at the expense of other women? Why do they build trust and loyalty with men while refusing to form meaningful bonds with women? Why do female rivalries keep happening? What's it going to take to stop? The research below will help you better understand the root causes of internalized sexism so you can spot and resist it.

WHY WOMEN MAY NOT SUPPORT OTHER WOMEN

1. Women Are Held to a Higher Standard

In a study from the *Journal of Personality and Social Psychology*, the nonverbal cues of an audience were studied when male and female leaders were speaking. Findings showed that both men and women judged female leaders more harshly. The study measured responses such as eye contact, body posture, and pleased versus displeased facial expressions as well as attribution of personality traits. For example, participants assigned men traits such as intelligence, skill, and ability, whereas women were seen as bossy, sensitive, and emotional. Subjects expressed a desire for women to "contribute less."[93] Additional research published in the *British Journal of Management* shows that female employees hold female managers to different standards than male managers.[94] Female bosses who behave in a traditionally managerial way, or "like a man," are likely to be rejected, while the same behavior is accepted and praised in male managers. Gallup reporting shows that 48% of Americans say they would prefer to work for a man rather than a woman, while 22% would choose a female boss and 28% do not care one way or the other. Surprisingly, men are more likely than women to say a boss's gender doesn't matter.[95]

2. Women Are Still Surrounded by Outdated Stereotypes

Women keep old-fashioned standards and stereotypes in place when they teach girls what is (and isn't) appropriate behavior. Tet says her mom told her to be an unquestioning "Yes" woman, but she simply couldn't do it. It went against her nature to be silent and complicit. This shows how daughters can learn from mothers to follow society's expectations versus their own instincts. Women need to model healthy

93   Doré Butler and Florence L. Geis, "Nonverbal Affect Responses to Male and Female Leaders: Implications for Leadership Evaluations," Journal of Personality and Social Psychology 58, no. 1 (1990): 48–59, https://doi.org/10.1037/0022-3514.58.1.48.

94   Sharon Mavin, "Queen Bees, Wannabees and Afraid to Bees: No More Best Enemies for Women in Management?," SSRN Scholarly Paper (Rochester, NY: Social Science Research Network, February 26, 2008), https://papers.ssrn.com/abstract=1095907.

95   Wendy W. Simmons, "When It Comes to Choosing a Boss, Americans Still Prefer Men," Gallup.com, January 11, 2001, https://news.gallup.com/poll/2128/When-Comes-Choosing-Boss-Americans-Still-Prefer-Men.aspx.

relationships with other women so their daughters can learn what healthy relationships between women look like.[96] Aiko reminded me that praising women and role-modeling healthy relationships between women, especially in front of our daughters, is one of the best ways to counteract the cycle of mean girls and queen bees.

3. Women Don't Update Their Assumptions and Biases About Women's Competence

Cheryl makes sure to update her mindset and challenge her own negative assumptions. "A huge growth area for me as a black woman and especially a black woman in professional spaces was unconsciously not realizing how much I didn't think I deserved certain things. I had to deprogram myself of the past to believe I deserve as much as anybody else. I remind myself that I'm intelligent and know my shit." These personal mantras can be lifesavers.

The Next Gen women brought up a great point—women who are vocal about their talents and proficiencies are frequently disliked by other women. In the same breath, they talked about how conflict is OK for men, but women are supposed to be peacemakers. Having to be quiet and agreeable gets tiring, especially when women feel constantly judged for asserting themselves, sticking up for their success, or even just being confident.

---

96 Meghan Rose Donohue, Sherryl H. Goodman, and Erin C. Tully, "Positively Biased Processing of Mother's Emotions Predicts Children's Social and Emotional Functioning," *Early Childhood Research Quarterly* 38 (October 6, 2016): 1–9, https://doi.org/10.1016/j.ecresq.2016.08.006.

4. Not Enough Seats at the Table for Women—Still

We mentioned earlier how women CEOs and executive board members are greatly outnumbered by men. We also talked about how there's an idea that "only one seat" is available at the table for women. This gets confirmed by how a leadership team looks, and in the reality of who gets promoted. When you can see only one woman on a leadership team, it's reasonable to believe there's limited space for people who look like you.

> **LESLIE FEINZAIG** SAYS:
>
> "One seat at the table for women is a recipe for disastrous relationships. It promotes a scarcity mentality among women who aim for management- and director-level positions. Women can unwittingly reinforce this myth of scarcity by shutting out other women when they reach the top. This is prevalent with type A personalities and with older career women who grew up in corporate settings where 'one seat' was a reality. They were often told, 'We already have one of you on the team.'"

Ruchika shares, "Women have been my most positive influences and biggest champions, but I've been encouraged to have sharp elbows, instead of being collaborative with them." She spoke about a woman in upper management who kept telling the men who were in charge that Ruchika was too expensive, not worth it, and should be fired. Ruchika was encouraged to "work harder" to show this woman her worth, and to not make a big deal of it. She concluded that her drive and ambition could be a warning signal to other women. Companies with only "one seat" will foster competitive environments. Kieran Snyder says she's experienced more kindness from women at startups versus large corporations. She believes that when there's unlimited possibility as an entrepreneur, you are far less likely to view women as a threat to your progress.

Ending Rivalries and Joining Forces

Regardless of where you work, there are actions you can take to end female rivalries and join forces with your female colleagues.

Recognize (and Reject) Double Standards/Double Binds

Women, if there's one thing you get from this chapter, I hope it's encouragement to collaborate, even if you are competing with the women around you. Remember Adam Grant's supportive rivalry? This means examining your own bias against other women, seeing how you stereotype them, and realizing that if you sabotage the progress of women, you're ultimately sabotaging yourself. Your bias might surprise you or cause you to feel regret. Now that you're better informed, you can reject unwanted thoughts and make different, more intentional choices.

I've held myself and other women to unrealistically high expectations at times too. One of my female direct reports did far more than some of the men, but I realize now that I expected above-and-beyond performance from her. When it came time for her review, I rated her well but could have gone higher. I wanted to be fair, and even checked with two layers of management to ensure that I wasn't being overly harsh about the assignments she hadn't completed. Those leaders (who both happened to be women) agreed with me, but they likely were not aware of the unrealistically high expectations they too placed on female team members. There's a chance each of us on that team subconsciously believed women in senior roles must work even harder to be recognized and rewarded. Not only did we place this expectation on other women, but we assigned it to ourselves as well. We expected perfection. It's true for me—the tendency to relentlessly prove my worth showed up early in my career. I've since given up perfectionism for good enough, but I continuously have to check myself to see if I'm expecting perfect performance from other women. I ask myself: Would I treat a male colleague or direct report the same way?

To help uncover your own standards for women, ask yourself these questions:

Ensuring fair standards and expectations for female colleagues:

- Do you mistrust the women around you?
- Do you criticize women for minor transgressions and forgive men for major ones?
- Do you make excuses for men's behavior as "just the way it is"?
- Do you hold women to an artificially high standard?
- Do you compete more than you collaborate with female colleagues?

Ensuring fair standards and expectations of yourself:

- With whom do you silence yourself out of fear or protection?

- When do you feel pressured to be nice, even when you don't mean it?

- When do you say yes to more work when you have too much already?

- When do you stay silent because you don't think you have value to add?

- When do you take the blame to avoid anger or confrontation?

Set and Protect Your Boundaries

Remember the female VP who asked me to be silent in meetings? I realized she wasn't trying to cause harm. When I left the company, she was truly shocked and caught off guard. I thought to myself, "You treat me like I'm worthless. Why would I continue to work for you?" There are times when we assume everyone is operating based on logic, but that's not always true. Trying to make sense of people's behavior can be difficult because they have their own motives, fears, and insecurities. If someone close to me behaved this way, I'd ask what's going on and try to find a solution. But since we didn't have a trusting relationship and she had power over me, I chose to walk away. This was not a battle I wanted to pick. There's a coaching quote that I believe wholeheartedly: "Every relationship is co-created." We can only change a relationship by first changing our own behavior. Trying to change the other person is futile. We can, however, open up and be vulnerable, giving them the chance to relate to us differently.

Cheryl says, "Being authentic is about me being the expert, the one who knows about diversity. It means I will walk away from contracts if needed, I won't agree to email-only communication, I'll make sure no one is changing my slides or presentations, and I won't let people tell me what will and will not work." Cheryl mentions having theme music play in her head when she walks away from bad situations. Her favorites? "Ambition" by Wale, or "BOSS" by The Carters, depending on the situation. What's your fight song?

Fran Dunaway has experienced female competition but says it didn't matter. Fran's company TomboyX is all about liking yourself and being cool just as you are. It's positive and uplifting. Consumers sense that. She believes, "You don't have to tear anyone down because people and brands speak for themselves."

A NOTE ABOUT BOUNDARIES

When it comes to boundaries, know what situations offend you. What are your hot buttons? For me, it's when people take credit for other people's work. As a leader, your team should get credit when you succeed, and you take the blame if things go wrong. Once a female colleague took credit for work that I contributed to her project. An entire section for her proposal was completed by me. I never thought twice about helping and was happy to do it. In the end, she removed my name altogether, suggesting she'd done all the work. That was a bridge burner, and I suspect she knows why I stopped spending time with her. I used to hold grudges until a friend reminded me it zaps your strength and energy. Now, I decide who is worthy of my time. Those people get my focused attention.

Heather Lewis had a female boss who showed noticeable insecurity about Heather's growth in the company. Heather's husband, Mikal, pointed out, "This isn't her problem. It's yours. She has control over your career." Heather had to make a strategic move to protect her position. Instead of pushing her career agenda, she put her needs on the back burner to build trust with this woman. She showed her tons of empathy and humbled herself, until the dynamic between them began to shift. It was draining, but it was the best option at the time.

Champion Women through Vocal and Public Support

Leslie founded her company on the basis of changing an important reality: "Women give each other advice. Men give each other deals." We have to start directing money and opportunities in women's direction, helping them pursue their ideas and launch sustainable companies. Fran is doing just that. "I am on board for generating wealth and then paying it forward to women and helping them find a way to do the same." With only 2% of the money from venture capital going to women, we can't wait for change.[97] We have to redirect the flow of wealth toward women, instead of just cheering them on and asking them to show up, as if that will solve the problem. Like the woman who cut Cheryl a check to help bootstrap her business. That was crucial to Cheryl's success and a great example of women's advocacy.

Shannon Anderson is the head of talent at Madrona Venture Group, a venture capital firm that invests in a number of my client companies. Since the day she started, my team has been included in their events and asked to present to their portfolio companies. Before

---

97   Valentina Zarya, "Female Founders Got 2% of Venture Capital Dollars in 2017," *Fortune*, January 31, 2018, http://fortune.com/2018/01/31/female-founders-venture-capital-2017/.

Shannon, I didn't see an opening to do such extensive work with Madrona. Now, we're at the table because she provided the seats. That's the kind of shift that can happen when there are women or male advocates in positions of power proactively helping those around them. As my company gets better known (and I have amazing advocates like Shannon), I'm included in what felt before like a secret society. These are the events you don't know exist or don't know how to get invited to, until someone lends a helping hand. It takes someone like Shannon to start the virtuous cycle.

Recently Shannon did something brilliant. When a woman in her network, Nicole Maddox, launched a new recruiting company called Flywheel Talent Strategy, Shannon called a few women entrepreneurs together to help Nicole brainstorm about branding and marketing. She asked us to share what we had learned while launching our businesses. In just an hour, we were able to provide concrete support that many women entrepreneurs never get. This is why Leslie Feinzaig started a platform where women could create opportunities for one another, just as men do.

Mar Brettmann reminds women to amplify each other, based on what she learned about President Obama's campaign. When women on the president's team felt they weren't being heard in meetings, they made a pact. If a woman's comment or idea was ignored, another woman would back her and repeat what she said. I've had women and men support me this way, too. When Jerry Hunter, now SVP Engineering at Snap, Inc., was my client at Amazon, he always knew when I had something to say. In the fast-paced executive meetings, I sometimes found it hard to get a word in or questioned the value of my comments. Jerry could tell just by looking at me when I was holding back and made it a habit to ask if I had something to contribute. Without him, many of my ideas would never have been heard.

You too can take note of who's been silent in meetings. Ask if they have anything they'd like to say. An invitation to speak can be a relief to those who aren't used to asserting themselves or have trouble jumping in. Better yet, slow down the conversation so that everyone has the chance for equal airtime.

In the Female Founders Alliance, female founders and CEOs help support each other with business opportunities, peer support, and camaraderie. Because Leslie couldn't find an organization like this when she needed one, she built her own. I too had unfavorable experiences in more than one CEO peer-learning organization. As a female business owner, established CEO peer groups didn't meet my needs, and I heard the same from other women I know.

> *"When women feel truly connected, there's a sense of comfort that allows for diverse perspectives and healthy competition."*

That's why I started an informal group of women in services (WISE). We've found that we benefit differently when talking to other women who have similar goals and challenges. Surrounding yourself with the right women creates a safe space like no other. Emily Parkhurst belongs to a group called the International Women's Forum, where everyone's in a managerial position. They're not in the same industries, but they're all managers who deal with teams, families, and career decisions. Several of the members have become her good friends.

Teri mentions a woman who emerged out of the blue to help grow her business. She says, "I've met her twice, and I feel like I've known her forever. She's a massive entrepreneur and angel investor. Super smart and just stellar. Her generosity blows my mind. She's helping me plan out my business over the next 10 years."

When women feel truly connected, there's a sense of comfort that allows for diverse perspectives and healthy competition. When women are connected inside a company, business leader Anne Welsh McNulty says, "It reduces the feeling of competition for an imaginary quota at the top. It helps other women realize, 'Oh, it's not just me'—a revelation that can change the course of a woman's career. It's also an indispensable way of identifying bad actors and systemic problems within the company."[98]

It's time for women to come together at work, for the sake of our success and well-being. Those of us who are mothers don't want our daughters to become mean girls, and we don't want them to be bullied or held back because of their gender. We want to role-model the power and kindness of women and show the world the strength we have when we join forces.

---

98   Anne Welsh McNulty, "Don't Underestimate the Power of Women Supporting Each Other at Work," *Harvard Business Review*, September 3, 2018, https://hbr.org/2018/09/dont-underestimate-the-power-of-women-supporting-each-other-at-work.

END-OF-CHAPTER CHECKLIST:
SEND THE ELEVATOR BACK DOWN!

Mid-Career and Next Gen Women:

☐   Send the elevator back down! If you've already "made it," don't unintentionally haze other women by putting them through the same challenges you faced over the course of your career.

☐   If you're a younger woman in the workplace, consider what you can learn from those who have been working longer than you. Recognize the battles they've faced, and what they've had to overcome.

☐   Join forces with other women to ask for what you collectively need at work. Working together is a proven way to influence leaders and effect change.

☐   Help women through mentorship, advocacy, and creating opportunities. You can redefine how women interact at work by proving there's room for many.

☐   Stop expecting more from female versus male bosses, peers, and direct reports. Stop judging women, including yourself, using a double standard.

Male Advocates:

☐   Make sure women are represented. When you see work groups, task forces, or project teams with only one woman or none, challenge the composition. Don't participate on *manels* (all-male panels); instead, demand that women join the group. Remember, diverse teams perform better across industries.[99]

☐ Hold all leaders, managers, and employees to equally high but realistic expectations, men and women both. Review your expectations and root out hidden gender bias.

☐ Discourage the "one seat at the table" practice and myth. Watch for and call out people who encourage rivalry versus collaboration among women.

HR, DEI, and Other Business Leaders:

☐ Intentionally create multiple seats at the table in senior leadership, managerial roles, and on cross-functional teams. Give talented women equal access to key, influential positions.

☐ Encourage and reward collaboration so that both women and men are incentivized to help (not hinder) each other's performance and progress.

☐ Introduce topics like mindfulness, emotional intelligence (EQ), and collaborative conflict that help all employees increase self-awareness and learn to treat others with respect.

---

99   https://hbr.org/2016/11/why-diverse-teams-are-smarter, https://www.forbes.com/sites/karstenstrauss/2018/01/25/more-evidence-that-company-diversity-leads-to-better-profits/#4894c5a21bc7

17

#MOMTOO

We have another battle to face in the workplace: parental discrimination. Becoming a mother has been the most amazing adventure of my life, and my career still continues to be a priority for me. It's time to talk about motherhood at work—before, during, and after pregnancy. We'll dive into the daily challenges mothers face and the policy changes that are long overdue. We'll explore how we can value working moms for their contributions and better support them as talented, capable, and critical members of any organization.

Before having kids, my definition of work–life balance was radically different. I was working as a technical recruiter, putting in long hours on top of a grueling commute. I cared deeply about my clients, and I knew job vacancies were tough on them. My husband Henry and I were in our twenties, and if we had dinner together at 8:00 or 9:00 p.m., it worked out fine. Some winters, it seemed I barely saw the light of day, but it didn't matter because my personal life was relatively simple, and I was satisfied spending a lot of time and energy on my career. It was all about my own priorities, boundaries, and expectations.

Fast-forward several years when my son Simon arrived. My workload and commute were the same, but like any new mom, I had more to juggle. I treated my first year back at work after Simon's birth as an experiment. I would do the best I could and see what happened. If I couldn't perform well *and* care for my baby, I was prepared to leave the company. Miraculously, everything worked out.

During those first few years when I was too tired to read *The New Yorker* or go out on Friday nights, I asked my friend and colleague Megan Morreale about life as a working mom. She said, "It doesn't work every day, but it works." Her reassuring advice

> *"It doesn't work every day, but it works."*

steadied me over the years, particularly because she was a tenured and successful mother of three. Before my kids were born, I hear women make self-deprecating jokes, calling themselves "bad moms" because quality time meant answering email on the couch while the kids sat beside them watching Disney movies. I swore I'd leave any job before I ever felt that way about myself as a parent. Once I became a working parent, I understood more clearly the choices parents are forced to make when work and family feel at odds.

Three years later when my daughter arrived, the thought of returning to work with two kids was daunting. I was given flexibility to leave early and work more from home. Some might call this the *mommy track*, a chance to step back for a few years. I was grateful and fortunate to receive such an opportunity. I tried but eventually rejected it. As an HR business partner, much of my work required face-to-face and ad hoc meetings that I couldn't do well with my partial work-from-home schedule. That was a real struggle for me. I "wanted it all" and believed it was attainable. I did not want to slow down or take a less challenging role just because I was a mom. Within a few months, the writing was on the wall. I could either strike a healthy work–life balance and feel I wasn't there for my clients, or I could pack up and find a company that didn't require quite so much of me. The week my resignation was announced, someone asked if I'd be working part-time instead. I answered no. I'd accepted a full-time job at Starbucks headquarters that was a short drive from home, and I would be working closer to forty, rather than sixty-plus, hours a week.

Today, I feel lucky to have personal interests, a successful business, and plenty of time with my husband and kids. My compassion for working moms has skyrocketed, and parenthood has energized me to do my part in breaking stereotypes and redefining unrealistic standards that so many corporations have placed on working mothers. Still, I wonder if my earlier jobs had been about 25% less demanding, whether I'd still be working in a big company today.

My kids have always known me as a career-driven mom. This prompted Sido, who adores children and is already thinking about her future, to ask, "Mom, is it bad if I want to have kids and stay home to raise them?" I told her the only bad choice is not being true to herself, and that she should do what makes her happy. I don't want her to think my career choices automatically apply to her or make me judgmental of her decisions. However, if she does take time off to have a family and later chooses to re-enter the workforce, I hope we will have reduced the obstacles that stand in the way of women today.

All but two of the thirteen women I interviewed are parents of biological children, stepchildren, or adopted children. Their stories, I noticed, had a common thread: Most of these women avoided or left corporate environments because the companies where they worked didn't offer the fairness and flexibility they needed. That's not a big surprise, considering the statistics.

Facts About Working Moms:

1. "40 percent of women with children under the age of 18 are also the primary breadwinners in their families. That's a figure that's made up mostly of single mothers, but it also includes a substantial share of married women."[100]

---

100 Janell Ross, "Most Americans Think Mothers Shouldn't Work Full-Time. The Reality Is Far Different," *The Washington Post*, accessed December 14, 2018, https://www. washingtonpost.com/news/the-fix/wp/2015/10/15/most-americans-think-mothers-shouldnt-work-full-time-the-reality-is-far-different/?utm_term=.d3861fc97b15.

2. "75 percent of working fathers think mothers *should not work* or should only work part-time in an ideal world. Seventy percent of them believe fathers with young children should still work full-time."[101]

3. Forty-three percent of women with children have voluntarily left work at some point in their careers. The #1 reason? More family time. Compare that to only 12% of men who voluntarily leave for the same reason.[102]

4. Data shows that women lose an average of 28% of their earning power when they take an "off-ramp." "Across sectors, women lose a staggering 37% of their earning power when they spend three or more years out of the workforce."[103] For each additional child a woman has, her earnings decrease 4%.[104]

5. "When job candidates were equal in every way except for a subtle indication that the candidate was a parent, being a mother reduced the chance that a candidate would be offered the job by 37 percentage points."[105]

6. "The recommended salary for mothers who were offered jobs was, on average, $11,000 less than what childless female candidates were offered."[106]

---

101 Ross, "Most Americans Think Mothers Shouldn't Work Full-Time."

102 Sylvia Ann Hewlett and Carolyn Buck Luce, "Off-Ramps and On-Ramps: Keeping Talented Women on the Road to Success," *Harvard Business Review*, March 1, 2005, https://hbr.org/2005/03/off-ramps-and-on-ramps-keeping-talented-women-on-the-road-to-success.

103 Hewlett and Buck Luce, "Off-Ramps and On-Ramps."

104 Michelle Budig, "The Fatherhood Bonus and The Motherhood Penalty: Parenthood and the Gender Gap in Pay," *Third Way*, September 2, 2014, https://www.thirdway.org/report/the-fatherhood-bonus-and-the-motherhood-penalty-parenthood-and-the-gender-gap-in-pay.

105 Katherine Goldstein, "Opinion | The Open Secret of Anti-Mom Bias at Work," *The New York Times*, May 16, 2018, https://www.nytimes.com/2018/05/16/opinion/workplace-discrimination-mothers.html.

106 Goldstein, "The Open Secret of Anti-Mom Bias at Work."

This explains why "the number of pregnancy discrimination claims filed annually with the Equal Employment Opportunity Commission has been steadily rising for two decades and is hovering near an all-time high."[107] Pressure is mounting, and yet corporate America has done very little to accommodate working moms. The US government has been equally unimpressive.

The Washington Post reports, "Twenty-five years ago President Bill Clinton signed the Family and Medical Leave Act [FMLA], which included a provision giving eligible workers 12 weeks of unpaid leave to care for a new child. Emphasis on 'unpaid.'" On top of that, the FMLA doesn't cover some 40% of the workforce. It's staggering to realize "the United States remains the only country in the developed world that does not mandate employer paid leave for new parents." Since we can't fix this voluntarily, mandating it is a good idea for any company large enough to pay.[108]

Pregnancy Discrimination Is Real, and It's Illegal

In May 2018, Katherine Chamberlain, who works along with my mother at law firm MacDonald, Hoague & Bayless, represented Danielle Stumpf, a paramedic whose employer subjected her to a hostile work environment based on her pregnancy, childbirth, and status as a nursing mother. A King County jury awarded her $415,000, due to "what a juror described after the verdict as a perfect storm of negative employment decisions" by AMR Ambulance Company. When Danielle Stumpf became pregnant and later stood up for her rights, a wave of discrimination and retaliation followed:

---

107 Natalie Kitroeff and Jessica Silver-Greenberg, "Pregnancy Discrimination Is Rampant Inside America's Biggest Companies," *The New York Times*, June 15, 2018, Business section, https://www.nytimes.com/interactive/2018/06/15/business/pregnancy-discrimination.html.

108 Christopher Ingraham, "Analysis | The World's Richest Countries Guarantee Mothers More Than a Year of Paid Maternity Leave. The U.S. Guarantees Them Nothing," *The Washington Post*, February 5, 2018.

- When Stumpf's doctor placed her on lifting restrictions and limited her to an eight-hour workday, the company forced her onto unpaid leave rather than giving her light-duty work during her pregnancy.

- While pregnant and on forced unpaid leave, the company excluded Stumpf from medical training classes. As a result, she was stripped of her seniority, which forced her to go back to working night shifts.

- When Stumpf returned to work after having her baby, the company refused to restore her to the field training officer position, a promotion she received before her pregnancy. She had to reapply three times over the next two and a half years to earn back the position.

- On a daily basis, there were harassing comments against Stumpf about her pump breaks, "including one comment that she should just 'hook a catheter to those things' instead of taking pump breaks. Witnesses testified at trial that male crew members complained about Stumpf taking breaks to pump milk for her baby and began referring to her as 'the milk truck.'"

- When Stumpf reported the harassment, AMR failed to put an end to these comments. Instead, the company instituted restrictive rules about where Stumpf could pump milk, forcing her to drive miles through traffic each day to pump at the company's main office, where she was subjected to ongoing harassment. The company caused Stumpf so much stress that her milk production stopped.

- Evidence presented at trial showed that Stumpf was not the only paramedic to have been mistreated after becoming pregnant.

After her trial, Danielle Stumpf said, "'I just want to thank the jury for approaching my case with an open mind and for reaching a just result. This means so much to me and my family, and I hope that AMR will change its practices to be more friendly to working mothers.'"[109] Because she's still at AMR near Tacoma, Washington, I assume they have improved. Yet what a costly way to make progress.

While Ruchika Tulshyan was pregnant, a CEO said to her, "In my experience, women have children and want to stay home. That's what my wife did." Can you see why that's unhelpful? It conveys a norm that's not the reality for many women. Oftentimes, professional men will use personal models (a wife, daughter, or mother) to justify how women should behave at work. They'll make assumptions that moms can't travel, work long hours, or handle high-visibility projects.

RUCHIKA TULSHYAN POINTS OUT:
"Because men make hiring, promotion, pay, or even funding decisions for female entrepreneurs, when they have this view of women with children, it literally ruins a woman's chances of getting ahead."

Men's assumptions symbolize their own outdated beliefs and ignorance about the range of choices, roles, and aspirations women have today.

Christy Johnson was brave to change jobs while she was pregnant. On her way into the new company, the second most powerful leader emailed the executive team announcing that a "massively pregnant lady" was coming to visit. Christy hadn't met them before, and this

---

109 "Jury Awards $415,000 to Paramedic for Pregnancy Discrimination," MacDonald, Hoague & Bayless, accessed December 14, 2018, https://www.mhb.com/cases/jury-awards-415000-to-paramedic-for-pregnancy-discrimination.

was her introduction as a new vice president. Christy says she experienced the most bias in her career when she was pregnant—from both men and women.

Kieran Snyder had a male colleague tell her she didn't get a promotion because she was pregnant. He was kind to tell her the truth, and he actually went to bat for her, but preconceived notions about working mothers disqualified her as a candidate. She didn't fight back. She just left the company.

> **KIERAN SNYDER** SAYS:
> "In general, when you're in a discriminatory environment, it's hard to fix it from within. For the average line employee without seniority, you'd have to find someone you trust to confide in, but it's easier just to leave. Just find a new job. Get a clean slate."

Given these experiences, it's no wonder many pregnant women leave companies or drop out of the workforce altogether. What would companies do if they had male turnover of this type? Why don't companies care when women leave? What is it that makes these companies continue forcing mothers to make impossible choices between work and family?

It's not surprising that in a *Harvard Business Review* study about why women leave the workforce, none of the women surveyed who were returning to their careers in business sectors wanted to rejoin their former employer—not a single one.[110] Imagine if those same employers

---

110 Hewlett and Buck Luce, "Off-Ramps and On-Ramps."

had shown more flexibility and understanding, what a difference it would have made. We talk about a war for talent saying companies can't hire fast enough, while at the same time we're disenfranchising a highly capable population. As women consider the companies they do want to work for, keep in mind that they have an informal network. Working mothers will ask one another about a company's reputation for equal treatment, work–life balance, and career growth, when considering job options.

Hitting the Maternal Wall

Once back on the job, moms face a mental and physical toll. Returning to work after childbirth, Christy Johnson says she felt more vulnerable than ever. Her motherhood was viewed as a weakness and used against her. She was subject to head games and manipulation. One female coworker, a self-professed expert in "helping women have it all," told Christy during their first meeting what she needed to do differently as a working mom. "You need to get an au pair. There is no way you and your husband can both work without a live-in nanny. It sounds like you bear most of the emotional labor; you definitely need to have a real conversation with your husband." Another woman asked if Christy "hated her children" for getting in the way of work. She was bombarded with unhelpful, judgmental comments like "I bet you miss your kids," or "My wife was a stay-at-home mom," or "My wife loved her job and she knew the right thing to do was to stay home with her kids." In Christy's situation, it started to become obvious that she wasn't able to be the 'team player' they needed her to be, which, of course, caused her to feel guilty. For instance, when she couldn't take business calls on Christmas Eve or jump on a plane unexpectedly, her worth to the company declined.

When I had my kids, stories circulated about women who famously responded to email from the hospital while in labor. They were praised for their dedication and for not missing a beat. At work, women often followed the arcane rule that children were not to be seen or heard during working hours, unless it was Halloween or bring your child to work day. I remember a colleague who would never say, "I'm taking care of a sick kid today." She'd claim she was ill because that seemed like a more acceptable excuse to her clients. We don't stop being mothers from nine to five, yet if we're needed by our children during those hours, it's viewed as a disruption to the organization. Contrast this with a senior engineer I knew. If there was snow in the mountains, he'd tell management they could find him on the slopes, not in his office. Everyone thought that was cool. He was never seen as a liability.

Heather mentioned an older male mentor who used to introduce her in meetings as a mom. Regardless of his intentions, which were unclear, it undermined her credentials. It didn't convey why she was in the room as a professional. Actress Amy Poehler vents a similar frustration. "'I have these meetings with really powerful men and they ask me all the time, "Where are your kids? Are your kids here?" . . . It's such a weird question. Never in a million years do I ask guys where their kids are.'"[111] Amy Nelson, founder of The Riveter, describes being rejected for a promotion after giving birth because her manager decided it "isn't the right time because you've just had a baby." Fear of himpathy prevented her from taking action or filing a complaint.[112]

---

111 Benjamin Svetkey, "Amy Poehler Is Really Making Herself Uncomfortable," Fast Company, May 11, 2015, https://www.fastcompany.com/3045739/amy-poehler-is-really-making-herself-uncomfortable.

112 Amy Nelson, "Perspective | Moms Are Punished in the Workplace, Even When We Own the Business," The Washington Post, January 29, 2018, https://www.washingtonpost.com/news/posteverything/wp/2018/01/29/i-started-my-own-business-i-still-couldnt-escape-stereotypes-about-working-moms/.

Who's Doing the Housework?

Another way that working mothers experience a disproportionate burden versus working fathers shows up in the home. When both parents work, housework is often left to the woman. This is referred to as a *double shift* or *second shift*. Studies show that women spend on average eighteen hours per week doing housework, while men average ten hours.[113] Same-sex couples aren't "immune from these sexist expectations" either. "In 2016, a revealing American study presented people with fictional accounts of gay and lesbian households, asking them to judge which partner ought to take responsibility for childcare, groceries, laundry and fixing the car. Reliably, respondents assigned the stereotypically female tasks to the partner described as having the more stereotypically feminine interests, such as a fondness for shopping or romantic comedies."[114]

It's Time Women and Men Put an End to This

Emily Parkhurst tells a story about a coworker who had to take vacation time to pump her breast milk. You heard that right. She wasn't allowed to just go to the restroom to take care of this essential task. "All of us were outraged. In addition to her feeling like '*Oh come on, are you serious?*' The rest of the women there thought it was insane. It's not lost on anybody that none of us work there anymore."

Tet Salva coined the term #MomToo to shed light on parental

---

113 Kim Parker and Wendy Wang, "Modern Parenthood: Roles of Moms and Dads Converge as They Balance Work and Family," Pew Research Center, March 14, 2013, http://www. pewsocialtrends.org/2013/03/14/chapter-5-americans-time-at-paid-work-housework-child-care-1965-to-2011/.

114 Oliver Burkeman, "Dirty Secret: Why Is There Still a Housework Gender Gap?," *The Guardian*, February 17, 2018, Inequality section, https://www.theguardian.com/inequality/2018/feb/17/dirty-secret-why-housework-gender-gap.

discrimination. She speaks publicly about how in some companies and corporate cultures mothers are seen as incompetent, unreliable, and mentally unstable. But the research shows just the opposite.[115] Through her research, Tet found that women are more productive when they return to work after having children. Other findings, however, were less encouraging.

"Ninety-eight percent of the women interviewed mentioned their careers experiencing a dramatic shift after having children; a majority of them could no longer attend the happy hours or company dinners where important connections and conversations take place. Some passed on special projects and looked for roles that didn't require a lot of travel. And there were a good number of women who left the corporate world all together to start their own businesses or go into consulting. The MomWarrior™ research also saw a shift in relationships after entering motherhood. Sixty-five percent of the women who focused on developing their relationships at home experienced diminished work relationships. The same is true for the opposite: the 25% who put in more time in developing relationships at work experienced weakened relationships at home, especially with their partners."[116]

Tet fights daily for mothers who get paid less than their female counterparts and highlights the link between purpose and parenthood. Tet also launched MomWarrior™ to provide knowledge, support, and a road map for working mothers who seek to thrive in all areas of life.

---

115 https://www.self.com/story/working-moms-productive-anyone-else, https://qz.com/802254/the-ultimate-efficiency-hack-have-kids/

116 Email from Tet Salva, subject line: "Tet Salva – Female Firebrands," March 31, 2019.

TET SALVA SAYS:

"If I am going to tell my four daughters they can be anything they want, then we should have the infrastructure, systems, and policies to support their careers and beyond."

In 2012, Anne-Marie Slaughter published a provocative article in *The Atlantic* about what it will take to achieve opportunity for women. As the first woman director of policy planning at the State Department, she found herself worrying about her teenage son who was struggling in school and skipping classes back home in Princeton, New Jersey. After two years, she chose to return home to her role at Princeton University, rather than take a job with the White House or the State Department. Slaughter had been commuting home only on weekends and wanted to be with her family. As the woman who had been doing it all—holding a high-powered job and raising a family—she wrote the article as part of her initiative to stop perpetuating what she came to see as a myth: that women can "have it all at the same time."[117] *The Seattle Times* responded with a piece debating whether working fathers truly have it better. They questioned if it's possible for men to achieve work–family balance, or if women actually have a slight advantage.[118] Research has found that men and women's work–family desires and challenges are remarkably similar. "It is what they experience at work once they become parents that puts them in very different places." For instance, "If men do ask, say,

117 Anne-Marie Slaughter, "Why Women Still Can't Have It All," *The Atlantic*, June 13, 2012, https://www.theatlantic.com/magazine/archive/2012/07/why-women-still-cant-have-it-all/309020/.

118 Harold Taw, "Debating Whether Fathers Can Have It All," *The Seattle Times*, July 13, 2012, https://www.seattletimes.com/opinion/debating-whether-fathers-can-have-it-all/.

for a lighter travel schedule, their supervisors may cut them some slack—but often grudgingly and with the clear expectation that the reprieve is temporary."[119] This is causing men to speak up for their rights too. Fathers also want more family time.

When I spoke to the Next Generation women, they noticed an automatic assumption by managers and colleagues that they'll want to have children. One woman said, "Don't assume I want to have a family. Ask me first!" If they decided to have children and continue their careers,

> *"Don't assume I want to have a family. Ask me first!"*

they worried about being expected to make sacrifices greater than their male partners. They feared having to give up more of their hobbies and personal lives, in order to raise kids and have a family.

Encouraging Suggestions for Expecting and Working Moms

Choose when and how you share the news

During both my pregnancies, I changed jobs internally at Microsoft. The first time, it was during my first trimester. I chose not to disclose the news of my pregnancy during my internal interviews or when I received the offer. My boss was a guy with kids. He had an all-female team, and several of his female direct reports had gone on maternity leave before, so he was completely unfazed when I eventually told him. By my next pregnancy, I had a new boss who offered me a promotion during my first trimester. Because I trusted, liked him as a person, and didn't want to put him in a difficult position, I shared that I was

---

119 Catherine H. Tinsley and Robin J. Ely, "What Most People Get Wrong About Men and Women," Harvard Business Review, May 1, 2018, https://hbr.org/2018/05/what-most-people-get-wrong-about-men-and-women.

expecting and would take the full five months of maternity leave. He responded, "Great, when can you start?" In both cases, I was extremely fortunate to have such understanding and supportive managers.

Did you know it's illegal for companies to discriminate against candidates based on pregnancy or caregiver status? That means questions in job interviews about whether you have children, their ages, who cares for them, and their daycare schedules are not permissible. Do you have to tell your manager once you know you're pregnant? No, there is no legal requirement to share the news at any particular point in your pregnancy. Most employees keep their condition to themselves until they're at least through the first trimester. When to tell your employer is a personal choice, not a legal one.

Practically speaking, you should evaluate your relationship and level of trust with your boss. Consider your company's track record of supporting expecting moms. When you're ready to tell them you're pregnant, it's ideal to talk to your boss in person in a focused discussion. Don't lump the news into an existing meeting or catch your boss off guard. Prepare to talk about your due date, when you would like to start and end your maternity leave and ask who in HR can explain your company's benefits and leave policies. If you have ideas about who can cover your work while you're out, it's helpful to make recommendations and even think about creating a transition plan.

Be thoughtful about the order in which you let people know you're pregnant. Tell your boss before they hear it from someone else. If you're connected to your coworkers on social media, remember that news travels fast, and once you post, it's out of your control. If you're concerned that your boss will be negative or unsupportive, talk to HR first, so they can support you and ensure that you have access to company benefits, including paid time off for maternity leave.

Put on your oxygen mask first

Ruchika describes the concept of pouring from an empty cup, which originated with Eleanor Brownn. "Rest and self-care are so important. When you take time to replenish your spirit, it allows you to serve others from the overflow. You cannot serve from an empty vessel."[120] My own analogy comes from the emergency instructions on flights: Put on your oxygen mask before assisting others. How do you know when you need to take care of yourself? For me, it's when I'm so drained that I no longer have the energy to focus. That's when I know I need to take a break and relax. We have to know when our cup is empty or down to the dregs and take breaks to avoid exhaustion and burnout.

MALA SINGH CONFESSES:
"There's something about a hammock that transports me to another world."

Mala is choosy about how she spends her time and with whom. I asked if she ever feels guilty. Nope. She feels like a better mom for modeling that it's OK to take care of herself.

Mar, on the other hand, struggles with guilt, and so did most of the women I interviewed. She feels guilty for needing time to herself or not spending enough time with friends. She also feels guilty about wanting time away when her toddlers scream and fight. "It can drive me to drink," Mar jokes. "But seriously, the mornings when I wake up and do yoga, I find more inner patience and peace. Some mornings, it's like the kids pick up on that. But other mornings, little tantrum monsters fill

---

120 Brownn, "Welcome," Eleanor Brownn, accessed December 15, 2018, http://www. eleanorbrownn.com/.

their brains, and all I can do is try my best to be a steady point for them." I'm certain this is something every parent can relate to.

Because Kieran is a morning person, she runs or swims at the crack of dawn to feel her best. In the evenings and on weekends, she coaches her girls' basketball team, which she finds highly meditative.

KIERAN SNYDER SAYS:
"There's no choice than to be fully present."

Whether you enjoy physical activities, getting outdoors, or curling up with a book, it's important to take time off and care for yourself. Make your needs a priority. It'll ultimately be good for the whole family. Self-care is not selfish; it's anything but.

Leverage your strengths as a working mom

Washington Post journalist Ylan Q. Mui writes, "A word of encouragement for my working moms: You are actually more productive than your childless peers. That's the conclusion of a recent study from the Federal Reserve Bank of St. Louis, which found that over the course of a 30-year career, mothers outperformed women without children at almost every stage of the game. In fact, mothers with at least two kids were the most productive of all."[121]

Both Christy and Mala improved their time management skills

---

121 Ylan Q. Mui, "Study: Women with More Children Are More Productive at Work," *The Washington Post*, October 30, 2014, https://www.washingtonpost.com/news/wonk/wp/2014/10/30/study-women-with-more-children-are-more-productive-at-work/?noredirect=on&utm_term=.e261fdcbd1a1.

and learned to set better boundaries after having kids. Mar gained leadership skills through parenting and says, "Some of the basic things I've learned in raising toddlers have taught me how to be a better manager of people. That's been an unexpected outcome." Mar observed that all people regardless of age have the same need to be treated with respect and dignity. With toddlers, the cause and effect are closely linked in time, making them simple to connect because a toddler reacts so quickly. You know if you're doing things right, creating an instantaneous feedback loop. "Or if you're not," says Mar, "the reaction is right there, and you know exactly the impact you've had."

> *"Mothers outperformed women without children at almost every stage of the game. In fact, mothers with at least two kids were the most productive of all."*

When a woman can feel powerful and productive at work, it benefits her children too. Studies have shown that for mothers, having authority and discretion at work was associated with mentally healthier children. "That is, we found that children benefit if their mothers have control over what happens to them when they are working.

> *"Some of the basic things I've learned in raising toddlers have taught me how to be a better manager of people. That's been an unexpected outcome."*

Further, mothers spending time on themselves—on relaxation and self-care—and not so much on housework, was associated with positive outcomes for children."[122]

---

122 Stewart D. Friedman, "How Our Careers Affect Our Children," *Harvard Business Review*, November 14, 2018, https://hbr.org/2018/11/how-our-careers-affect-our-children.

Change your expectations of mothers, including what you expect of yourself

At the end of my first day back at work after Simon was born, I felt so proud to have made it through the commute, plus a full day. At 5:00 p.m. sharp, I grabbed my coat and purse, and while heading for the door, a young woman said, "Only working a half-day?" This seemed so callous, like an intentional dig. I seethed on the way home, thinking how "congratulations" or "welcome back" would have been a kinder way to acknowledge the difficulty of that day. I was unprepared for how hard women are on working moms. Why make a trying time at work even more difficult?

Transitioning to and returning from maternity leave can be extremely difficult times for women, yet we act as if they should come and go as though it's any other day. I had mustered all of my strength to work eight hours and got criticized for it. A big part of making companies more friendly toward women means easing these transitions, as some companies are starting to do. Progressive companies are introducing gradual transitions back, lactation support, night nurses, and even contributing to child-care costs.

On my first day back from leave after Sidonie was born, the person who had been covering for the past five months had already begun her new role. Annual performance reviews were scheduled to kick off, a notoriously busy time for HR. Not to mention, I was given the lead role in several projects my manager had been driving. With no time to settle in, the speedometer went from zero to eighty. I came home in the evening too physically exhausted to hold my daughter. Is it any wonder that in less than five months I had found a new job, closer to home, with more reasonable hours?

Remember Heather's mentor who would introduce her at meetings as a mom? She wound up telling him that this introduction was no longer going to work. He said he had assumed she would appreciate the mom title because other women he knew liked it. She explained how it affected her, and he listened with a sense of caring. She realized he didn't know many young women at work, and Heather said it felt good to tell him how he could do an even better job for her and future women colleagues. He needed to update his approach and was happy to do so once he had the feedback.

Role-model life with kids

Kieran tells a story I love: "I have a daughter who is eight and two stepdaughters who are nine and seven. About two years ago, I was giving them a snack before bed, and I said jokingly, 'Hey, why don't you all stay up and do my work, and I'll go to bed?' The oldest is sweet. She just wants to save animals with her life. She asked, 'What work do you have to do?' I explained that I had to write a story, do a bunch of math, and call up some people and have an argument with them. The oldest said she would help with the story. The middle kid, who is the 'math girl,' agreed to do the math. The youngest said, 'I'll call up those people and argue with them until they give you what you want.' I was like, 'Wow, my team is right here!'"

Heather occasionally brings her five-year-old daughter Amala to work at Rover on the weekends. She feels comfortable there, which thrills Heather. Amala takes snacks and has a little standing desk, which the CEO made for her. Isn't that amazing? Heather says, "Her understanding of work and where women belong is being shaped by what she sees me do."

I lean toward intentional oversharing with my team when I take time off for family reasons. This is even more important to me because many prominent senior women, from Oprah Winfrey to Gloria Steinem, are kid-free. If I leave early on Friday afternoon to take Simon to a soccer tournament or Sido rock-climbing, or if I stay home when they're sick, rather than hiding what's taking place, I publicize why I'm not available. I want my team to know that I understand the challenges of balancing work and kids. I know our kids need us, and when they need us is often unplanned and unpredictable. I never want parents on my team to feel guilty about putting their family first.

Remember my colleague at Microsoft, Megan Morreale, who was a role model for me when I first had my kids? While she was always composed, she also shared funny stories like how she snuck ice cream every night after putting her kids to bed. She even had empty picture frames on her desk with Post-it notes reminding her to "Bring Pictures!" You may have done that too, but I want to be clear—she had those Post-it reminders on her frames the whole five years we worked together. It cracked me up. Since Megan had three kids ages six and under, she had all kinds of sayings to get her through the rough patches. One was that as long as she didn't have three bad days in a row, life was good.

Parental discrimination is real. It has detrimental effects both on organizations and on working moms. The impact even spreads to women who don't have children and aren't planning to, simply because one day they too might become mothers. While it's true for most women that becoming a working mom is hard work and requires a new kind of balance and flexibility, that is no reason to exclude moms from the workforce or limit their opportunities. Research shows that working moms are some of the most organized and productive employees around. Let's support women while they're expecting, as they transition and go on maternity leave and come back to work, and when their children need them. If working moms are willing to make sacrifices on behalf of their jobs, as they inevitably do, it's long past time they get the support and credit they deserve from their employers.

END-OF-CHAPTER CHECKLIST: #MOMTOO

Mid-Career and Next Gen Women:

☐ Paint an accurate picture of what it takes to be a working mom. Don't sugarcoat it or romanticize. Be honest about the benefits, challenges, and trade-offs.

☐ Talk to your partner about shared expectations in and outside of the home. Find ways to support each other and agree to flex when one of you is extra busy at work.

☐ Know your limits at work. List what sacrifices you are willing and unwilling to make as a parent. Will you travel? What if you occasionally miss dinner or bedtime; is that OK? Share your preferences with your manager and brainstorm solutions that work for both of you.

☐ Use suggestion boxes or company meetings to request more modern, family-friendly policies and benefits that reflect today's reality. Ask your colleagues to do the same. Remember, more voices result in attention and action.

☐ Familiarize yourself with your rights regarding pregnancy, parental leave, sick time, paid time off, and pumping at work. There's no shortage of resources available online.

☐ Seek out companies that support working moms. Use resources like *Working Mother's Annual 100 Best Companies* list. Research company policies to see what kind of parental leave, remote work options, and benefits they offer.

Male Advocates:

☐   Speak up when you hear assumptions being made about women, such as that they're definitely going to want kids, quit their jobs, or not return from maternity leave.

☐   Don't judge the mothers in your life for their choices, whether that's taking time off, working full-time or part-time, or not knowing what they want to do. These are difficult decisions. Women deserve your support, patience, and understanding.

☐   Dads: Take paternity leave, if it's offered. If not, ask for it. The more men take advantage of this benefit and normalize it, the less women will be stigmatized.

HR, DEI, and Other Business Leaders:

☐   Train interviewers and hiring managers to make decisions based on qualifications, not gender. Make sure they know questions about pregnancy, parental status, and childcare arrangements are illegal and irrelevant.

☐   Institute flexible work benefits that support not just women, but also men and people without children. Offer part-time positions, job shares, work-from-home and remote work options. You'll be surprised at how this helps you attract and retain talented employees from all walks of life.

☐   Update leave policies for parents, including equal maternity and paternity leave, and incentives for new parents to take time off. Offer benefits for non-traditional families including paid time off and bonding time for adoptions and surrogacy leave.

18

EVERY LITTLE
STEP MATTERS

I want to thank you for spending time with this book. Together, we took a hard look at the root of privilege and how it gets in the way of inclusion at work. We examined the momentum of the #MeToo movement, which has given us new language to talk about what women face at work and what we will no longer tolerate. We learned to speak up for ourselves, advocate for others, and influence organizations to consider the needs and rights of women. We also discussed the unfortunate reality of female rivalry, and new ways to mix healthy competition with support and collaboration. We learned how all genders hold women to unrealistically high standards, how we fight unnecessarily for limited seats at the table, and how we can all do better for ourselves and each other. We recognized our strengths as working moms and reviewed strategies about how to accommodate mothers and, by extension, all parents.

No matter where you work, regardless of your profession or years in business, it's now your responsibility to take advantage of what you've learned. Did you know that if you commit to your goals by sharing them with someone else, you have a 65% chance of meeting them? "And if you have a specific accountability appointment with a person you've committed, you will increase your chance of success by up to 95%."[123] Find an accountability partner and share at least one action you're committed to taking today. Every little step matters.

My hope for future generations stems from the language they've gained to name what they're experiencing. They have more tools and information than ever to insist that sexual harassment and discrimination have to stop. It took decades for us mid-career women to recognize inappropriate and illegal treatment. The Next Generation already sees this behavior for what it is. They're quicker and more adept at responding, holding people accountable, and walking away from unfair and discriminatory managers and organizations. I have complete faith that they'll learn to speak up for themselves or move on, and continue to vote with their feet.

This poem was written by my daughter's middle school classmate. She's expecting a lot from the world; things that at her age, I didn't even know were possible. Let's hope her generation of girls won't need a sledgehammer by the time they reach the workplace. And if they do, it's encouraging to know we've passed down at least a little wisdom to help them get the job done.

---

123 Thomas Oppong, "This Is How to Increase the Odds of Reaching Your Goals by 95%," Medium (blog), January 16, 2017, https://medium.com/the-mission/the-accountability-effect-a-simple-way-to-achieve-your-goals-and-boost-your-performance-8a07c76ef53a.

PANTOUM OF THE GLASS CEILING

Society says that there is a glass ceiling.

Our world says, womxn can't break through.

It blocks opportunity.

Above it there is a blinding white world.

Our world says, womxn can't break through.

All womxn should be born with a sledgehammer to smash through that glass.

Above it there is a blinding white world.

All we want is gender equality.

All womxn should be born with a sledgehammer to smash through that glass.

Equality is nonexistent below.

All we want is gender equality.

Womxn's rights are human rights.

Equality is nonexistent below.

It blocks opportunity.

Womxn's rights are human rights.

Society says that there is a glass ceiling.

By Sabina Baumgardner, age 13

GLOSSARY

Some terms in this book might be new to you. I attempted to explain them throughout the book. The language of diversity, equity, and inclusion is growing; new words and phrases are frequently adopted. You'll find these words in italics throughout the book and can come here for definitions.

Advocate—(verb) In a work setting, to use one's position of relative power and privilege to ensure that a colleague is noticed, respected, and given credit for their contributions. (noun) A person who uses his/her power as described above.

Ally—A person who uses their privilege to support groups or individuals without that privilege. Being an ally is not an identity, but rather an active practice of solidarity with marginalized people.[124]

Amplify—To make someone else's voice and ideas heard when they might otherwise be silenced, ignored, or excluded. Examples include repeating comments while giving credit to the original speaker to ensure she is heard, or asking questions to create space for someone to speak by giving them the floor.

Bystander—A person who is present while someone else is the target

---

124 "Guide to Allyship," accessed December 8, 2018, http://www.guidetoallyship.com/;
"What Is Allyship? Why Can't I Be an Ally?," *PeerNetBC* (blog), November 22, 2016,
http://www.peernetbc.com/what-is-allyship.

of harassment, discrimination, or violence. Although the word has a passive connotation, bystanders have the opportunity to mitigate damage to a victim by intervening during or after an incident (Also see "Upstander").[125]

Cisgender—Referring to a person whose "sense of personal identity and gender corresponds with their birth sex."[126]

Concrete ceiling—A barrier limiting the advancement of women of color in organizations. "The metaphor of a 'concrete ceiling' stands in sharp contrast to that of the 'glass ceiling.' Not only is the 'concrete ceiling' reported to be more difficult to penetrate, women of color say they cannot see through it to glimpse the corner office."[127]

Culture—Any variety of norms; the way we do things around here. May apply to clothing, language, hierarchy, decision-making, accepted behaviors, and so on. Whether or not it's written down, every company has a culture.

Diversity—Diversity is "the presence of difference within a given setting." One person cannot be "diverse."[128] Diversity can include skin

---

125 "Bystander Intervention Resources," *Hollaback! Together We Have the Power to End Harassment* (blog), accessed December 8, 2018, https://www.ihollaback.org/resources/bystander-resources/.

126 Oxford, s.v. "cisgender," accessed December 8, 2018, https://en.oxforddictionaries.com/definition/cisgender.

127 "Women of Color Report a 'Concrete Ceiling' Barring Their Advancement in Corporate America," *Catalyst*, July 13, 1999, https://www.catalyst.org/media/women-color-report-concrete-ceiling-barring-their-advancement-corporate-america.

128 Meg Bolger, "What's the Difference Between Diversity, Inclusion, and Equity?," *GA Blog* (blog), October 24, 2017, https://generalassemb.ly/blog/diversity-inclusion-equity-differences-in-meaning/.

color, country of origin, gender, sexual orientation, and many other attributes, both seen and unseen.

Diversity, Equity, and Inclusion (DEI)—"Diversity, Equity, and Inclusion is a collective process that specializes in the building of safe and empowering policies and practices through the existence of diverse identities, in safe and welcoming spaces, that results in fair outcomes."[129]

Double bind—"Because women are often evaluated against a masculine standard of leadership, women are left with limited and unfavorable options, no matter how they behave and perform as leaders." For instance, women can be perceived as "too soft or too tough but never just right."[130]

Double shift (also known as second shift)—When women who work outside of the home are responsible for domestic duties and caregiving at home, more so than their male partners. They experience double the pressure.[131]

Double standard—"A set of principles that applies differently and usually more rigorously to one group of people or circumstances than to another; especially a code of morals that applies more severe standards of sexual behavior to women than to men."[132]

Employee Resource Group (ERG)—"Employee Resource Groups

129 Cheryl Ingram, email to author, December 11, 2018.

130 "The Double-Bind Dilemma for Women in Leadership: Damned If You Do, Doomed If You Don't," *Catalyst*, October 24, 2012, https://www.catalyst.org/knowledge/double-bind.

131 https://www.dailymail.co.uk/femail/article-1342843/How-women-suffer-double-shift-stress-home-AND-work.html

132 Merriam-Webster, s.v. "double standard," accessed December 10, 2018, https://www.merriam-webster.com/dictionary/double+standard.

(ERGs) are voluntary, employee-led groups that foster a diverse, inclusive workplace aligned with organizational mission, values, goals, business practices, and objectives."[133]

Equity—"Equity is an approach that ensures everyone access to the same opportunities." Equity recognizes advantages and barriers and is "a process that begins by acknowledging that unequal starting place and continues to correct and address the imbalance."[134]

Feminism—The belief in and advocacy for women's rights in order to achieve social and political equality between women and men. Historically, white women have used feminism to advocate for women's rights in a way that was not inclusive of the additional layers of oppression experienced by women of color. (For an alternative, see "Intersectional feminism.")

Feminist—One who advocates for women's rights and believes in equality for all genders. People of all genders can be feminists.

Firebrand—"A person who is passionate about a particular cause," typically inciting change and taking radical action.[135]

Gaslighting—Manipulating someone "by psychological means into doubting their own sanity."[136]

---

133 "ERGs (Employee Resource Groups)," *Catalyst*, accessed December 10, 2018, https://www.catalyst.org/knowledge/topics/ergs-employee-resource-groups.

134 Bolger, "What's the Difference Between Diversity, Inclusion, and Equity?"

135 Oxford, s.v. "firebrand," accessed December 10, 2018, https://en.oxforddictionaries.com/definition/us/firebrand.

136 Oxford, s.v. "gaslight," accessed December 10, 2018, https://en.oxforddictionaries.com/definition/gaslight.

Gender pay equity—"Pay equity is equal pay for work of equal value. Equal pay for equal work addresses situations in which men and women do the same work."[137]

Gender pay gap—"The gender pay gap or gender wage gap is the average difference between the remuneration for men and women who are working [across all jobs]. Women are generally paid less than men."[138] Women of color are generally paid less than white women.

Glass ceiling—"An unacknowledged barrier to advancement in a profession, especially affecting women and members of minorities."[139]

Glass cliff—A phenomenon where women and minority groups who do break through the glass ceiling end up in leadership positions with a higher risk of scrutiny, criticism, and failure.[140]

Hepeating—When women's ideas are repeated by men in meetings without giving credit.[141]

---

137 "Pay Equity and Equal Pay: What Is the Difference? | Pay Equity Commission," accessed December 10, 2018, http://www.payequity.gov.on.ca/en/AboutUs/Pages/the_difference.aspx.

138 "Gender Pay Gap," *Wikipedia*, December 8, 2018, https://en.wikipedia.org/w/index.php?title=Gender_pay_gap&oldid=872742765.

139 Oxford, s.v. "glass ceiling," accessed December 10, 2018, https://en.oxforddictionaries.com/definition/glass_ceiling.

140 "The Glass Cliff," July 27, 2011, https://web.archive.org/web/20110727233341/http://psy.ex.ac.uk/seorg/glasscliff/.

141 Nicole Gugliucci, "My Friends Coined a Word: Hepeated. For When a Woman Suggests an Idea and It's Ignored, but Then a Guy Says Same Thing and Everyone Loves It," Tweet, *@NoisyAstronomer* (blog), September 22, 2017, https://twitter.com/NoisyAstronomer/status/911213826527436800?ref_src=twsrc%5Etfw%7Ctwcamp%5Etweetembed%7Ctwterm%5E911213826527436800 &ref_url=https%3 A%2F%2F www.businessinsider.com%2Fwhat-is-hepeating-2017-9.

Himpathy—"The inappropriate and disproportionate sympathy powerful men often enjoy in cases of sexual assault, intimate partner violence, homicide, and other misogynistic behavior."[142]

Himpunity—A cultural habit of letting men off the hook for harmful actions, including serious crimes, especially when those actions have harmed a woman.[143]

Inclusion—The embrace of people with different identities such that they feel and are "valued, leveraged, and welcomed within a given setting (e.g., your team, workplace, or industry)."[144]

Internalized sexism—The involuntary internalization by women of the sexist messages that are present in their societies and culture.

Intersectionality—The theory of how different types of discrimination interact to create a greater impact on those with multiple marginalized identities, specifically black women.[145]

Intersectional feminism—A form of feminism that advocates for all women, with particular regard for the differences between women

---

142 Kate Manne, "Opinion | Brett Kavanaugh and America's 'Himpathy' Reckoning," *The New York Times*, September 26, 2018, https://www.nytimes.com/2018/09/26/opinion/brett-kavanaugh-hearing-himpathy.html.

143 "Duke Univ Produces 'Himpathy,' 'himpunity' Podcast," *Campus Reform*, https://www.campusreform.org/?ID=11555.

144 Bolger, "What's the Difference Between Diversity, Inclusion, and Equity?"

145 Bim Adewunmi, "Kimberlé Crenshaw on Intersectionality: 'I Wanted to Come up with an Everyday Metaphor That Anyone Could Use,'" *New Statesman America*, April 2, 2014, https://www.newstatesman.com/lifestyle/2014/04/kimberl-crenshaw-intersectionality-i-wanted-come-everyday-metaphor-anyone-could.

related to race, sexuality, nationality, economic status, language, and other aspects of identity.[146]

LGBTQIA+—An acronym for Lesbian, Gay, Bisexual, Transgender, Queer (or Questioning), Intersectional, Asexual, and all other orientations or genders. The + represents inclusion of the many additional ways that a person may self-identify.

Manel—A panel of speakers or presenters that is all male, therefore not diverse or inclusive.

Mansplaining—To explain something to a woman in a condescending way that assumes she has no knowledge about the topic.

Maternal wall—A discrimination-based barrier to employment or career advancement faced by working mothers.[147]

Mentor—"A mentor at work is that special someone who is passionate about their career, has leadership experience, and has the wisdom only experience can provide."[148] A mentor volunteers his/her time to develop others.

---

146 "What Is Intersectional Feminism? A Look at the Term You May Be Hearing a Lot," *USA TODAY*, January 19, 2017, https://www.usatoday.com/story/news/2017/01/19/feminism-intersectionality-racism-sexism-class/96633750/.

147 Amy Nelson, "Perspective | Moms Are Punished in the Workplace, Even When We Own the Business," *Washington Post*, January 29, 2018, https://www.washingtonpost.com/news/posteverything/wp/2018/01/29/i-started-my-own-business-i-still-couldnt-escape-stereotypes-about-working-moms/.

148 Catherine Adenle, "10 Concrete Reasons Why Everyone Needs a Mentor at Work," *LinkedIn* (blog), November 24, 2014, https://www.linkedin.com/pulse/20141124121303-47571147-10-concrete-reasons-why-everyone-needs-a-mentor-at-work/.

#MeToo—The MeToo movement (or #MeToo movement), with many local and international alternatives, is a movement against sexual harassment and sexual assault.

Microaggressions—"Everyday verbal, nonverbal, and environmental slights, snubs, or insults, whether intentional or unintentional which communicate hostile, derogatory, or negative messages to target persons based solely upon their marginalized group membership."[149]

Mommy track—A career path for women with family responsibilities that de-prioritizes or impedes career advancement due to the assumption that mothers are less able or willing to make their career a priority.

Office housework—Non-promotable tasks that do not advance your career, like organizing a holiday party or serving on a low-ranking committee.[150]

Oppression—The abuse of power to "disempower, marginalize, silence or otherwise subordinate" based on social group or category, usually to benefit and increase the privilege of the oppressor.[151] "For every privilege, there is an oppression" (Cheryl Ingram).

Patriarchy—"Patriarchy is a social system in which men hold

149 Derald Wing Sue, "Microaggressions: More Than Just Race," *Psychology Today*, November 17, 2010, http://www.psychologytoday.com/blog/microaggressions-in-everyday-life/201011/microaggressions-more-just-race.

150 Linda Babcock, Maria P. Recalde, and Lise Vesterlund, "Why Women Volunteer for Tasks That Don't Lead to Promotions," *Harvard Business Review*, July 16, 2018, https://hbr.org/2018/07/why-women-volunteer-for-tasks-that-dont-lead-to-promotions.

151 "What Is Anti-Oppression?," *THE ANTI-OPPRESSION NETWORK* (blog), December 7, 2011, https://theantioppressionnetwork.com/what-is-anti-oppression/.

primary power." It asserts that males "predominate in roles of political leadership, moral authority, social privilege and control of property."[152]

Pence effect—The controversial idea of avoiding women at work to head off accusations of harassment; named for US vice president Mike Pence, who said he avoids dining alone with any woman other than his wife.[153]

Privilege—Unearned societal advantage that is only available to a particular group. Privilege can apply to many areas, including race, sex, sexuality, social class, ability, and age, and one person can have privilege in some areas while being oppressed in others.

Pronoun—In conversations about inclusion, "pronoun" typically refers to gender pronouns—a person's chosen pronouns such as *she*, *they*, or *he*—to refer to their gender identity. Being mindful of a person's preferred pronouns is an important aspect of inclusion.

Sexism—"Prejudice or discrimination based on a person's sex or gender. Sexism can affect anyone, but it systematically and primarily affects women and girls."[154]

Sponsor—(noun) Someone within an organization's inner circle of influence who sees the strengths and potential of a more junior or

---

152 Wikipedia Contributors, "Patriarchy," *Wikipedia*, December 10, 2018, https://en.wikipedia.org/w/index.php?title=Patriarchy&oldid=873062932.

153 Gillian Tan and Katia Porzecanski, "Wall Street Rule for the #MeToo Era: Avoid Women at All Cost," *Bloomberg News*, December 3, 2018, https://www.bloomberg.com/news/articles/2018-12-03/a-wall-street-rule-for-the-metoo-era-avoid-women-at-all-cost.

154 Wikipedia Contributors, "Sexism," *Wikipedia*, December 3, 2018, https://en.wikipedia.org/w/index.php?title=Sexism&oldid=871742707.

less visible employee and advocates for that person's recognition and career advancement with others in power.

Stereotype threat—The fear that you will conform to a stereotype about a group to which you belong, often leading to underperformance caused by anxiety and internalization of the stereotype.[155]

Systemic cultural reality—A truth that is ingrained and reinforced throughout society, in this case referring to white privilege.

#TimesUp—Time's Up is a movement against sexual harassment and discrimination in the workplace and was founded by Hollywood celebrities in response to the Weinstein effect and #MeToo.[156]

Underrepresented minority (URM)—Someone whose racial or ethnic identity is not represented in a given setting (i.e., a company or industry) in proportion to their percentage of the general population. URM is often defined differently depending on the context/industry. In this book, we talk a great deal about the tech industry, where underrepresented groups typically include people with disabilities, and racial and ethnic groups—blacks, Hispanics, American Indians, Alaska Natives, Pacific Islanders, Native Hawaiians, and those of two or more races.

Upstander—A bystander who takes positive action by speaking up or intervening on behalf of someone who is being mistreated, harassed, or bullied.

---

155 Wikipedia Contributors, "Stereotype Threat," *Wikipedia*, November 29, 2018, https://en.wikipedia.org/w/index.php?title=Stereotype_threat&oldid=871125248.

156 Alix Langone, "#MeToo and Time's Up Founders Explain the Difference Between the 2 Movements," *Time*, March 8, 2018, http://time.com/5189945/whats-the-difference-between-the-metoo-and-times-up-movements/.

Venture capital—A type of financing provided by investors to early stage companies and small businesses with high-growth potential, often in exchange for equity in the company. These investors are called venture capitalists.[157]

Victim blaming—Victim blaming is blaming the victim for a crime they didn't commit. Victim blaming is being blamed for somebody else's actions. For instance in rape cases, people in power such as the police, judge, or counselor ask the victim what they were wearing and whether they were drinking, as if those behaviors caused a crime to be committed against them.[158]

White fragility—Referring to the defensive moves that white people make when challenged racially, white fragility is characterized by emotions such as anger, fear, and guilt, and by behaviors including argumentation and silence. *The New York Times* best-selling book with this title by Robin DiAngelo explores the counterproductive reactions white people have when their assumptions about race are challenged, and how these reactions maintain racial inequality.

Womxn—A commonly used substitute to "women" to avoid using the suffix "-men." "Womyn" was originally coined as a substitute, but because the term was used in a way that intentionally excluded trans women, womxn is meant to be a more inclusive term.[159]

---

157 Investopedia Staff, "Venture Capital," Investopedia, accessed December 11, 2018, https://www.investopedia.com/terms/v/venturecapital.asp.

158 https://www.urbandictionary.com/define.php?term=victim%20blaming

159 Gwendolyn Wu, "Why Are People Using the Terms 'Womyn' and 'Womxn' Instead of 'Women'?," HelloFlo, March 23, 2016, http://helloflo.com/gwendolyn-women-etymology/.

FEMALE FIREBRANDS FREE ONLINE RESOURCES

It is my sincere hope that if you are a CEO, executive, team manager, HR, people operations, DEI, or other business professional, you will want to use what you learned to increase belonging and create an even better experience for women and all employees in your workplace. I've compiled a number of informative, actionable resources that will help you get started. Just go to the Female Firebrands website (https://reverbpeople.com/femalefirebrands/) to find research, checklists, and tools that you can use immediately.

You will also find several consulting firms that specialize in topics including advocacy and allyship, bystander training, removing bias from interviewing and hiring, closing the gender pay gap, pregnancy and parenthood at work, building healthy culture, and more.

In addition, you can download the end-of-chapter checklists and take the "Are You an Advocate?" and "Are You a Firebrand?" quizzes.

ABOUT THE AUTHOR

 **MIKAELA KINER** is an experienced HR/people operations professional, founder/CEO, and executive coach. In 2015, Mikaela founded Reverb, a leading provider of flexible People Operations services for startups and fast-growing companies in the Pacific Northwest. Reverb's purpose is to help companies create healthy, inclusive culture that engages and inspires employees. The firm works with companies such as Juno Therapeutics, Wizards of the Coast, and Microsoft, as well as many early stage startups.

Mikaela believes that people can have fun and be productive at work every day, as long as they're happy, challenged, and feel a sense of belonging. Craving balance in her own life, Mikaela created Reverb to work with companies who need just-in-time HR help. In line with her mission, the Reverb team has the flexibility to do meaningful work while enjoying time outside of work for themselves and their families.

Prior to founding Reverb, Mikaela held HR leadership roles at Northwest companies including Microsoft, Starbucks, Amazon, PopCap Games, and Redfin. In addition to living for three years in India, she's worked with leaders throughout Europe and Asia. Mikaela enjoys coaching leaders at all levels and working with mission-driven organizations.

Mikaela holds a master's degree in HR with a Certificate in Organizational Development from the New School for Social Research. She's a certified executive coach with a credential from the International

Coaching Federation, and a certified practitioner of Brené Brown's Dare to Lead™ curriculum. A native Seattleite who grew up on Capitol Hill, Mikaela is married to Henry, a musician, artist, and teacher. Their two children, Simon and Sidonie, are good at challenging the status quo and are a constant source of learning and laughter.